BOOZE, BADBOYS
& BOOTLEGGERS

BOOZE, BADBOYS & BOOTLEGGERS

THE VIOLENT YEAR - 1921
(MORE NORTH COUNTRY TALES GRANDPA NEVER TOLD YOU)

VOLUME 2

JAMES E. REAGEN

ISBN: 979-8-9915766-8-0 (Paperback)
      979-8-9915766-9-7 (Hardcover)

Published by Oswegatchie Press

Interior design by Booknook.biz

TABLE OF CONTENTS

AUTHOR'S NOTE

want to thank everyone who bought copies of my first volume of Booze, Badboys and Bootleggers (North Country Tales Grandpa Never Told You). Frankly, I was overwhelmed by the wonderful response I received from families across Northern New York who purchased copies for themselves, their friends, and relatives.

Many people were shocked to learn their not-so-distant ancestors were once involved in bootlegging. Others were not surprised. Many always suspected that some of their ancestors got their start in the booze trade.

As the former Managing Editor of the Ogdensburg Journal and Advance News, I spent my career finding out about stories that people want to read. As someone who writes about North Country history, that is what I still try to do - tell stories from long ago that everyone will enjoy reading. What too many people from our region have trouble understanding is that history happened right here. It is up to us to preserve our local history and make sure that future generations celebrate and remember it.

I think our school history teachers should consider incorporating our colorful local historical events into their lessons about our national history. Too many grow up not realizing the last battle of the French and Indian War was fought off our shore, that what's now St. Lawrence and Jefferson County were British held territory during the Revolutionary War, that our local Civil War heroes helped end that war early, and that we were at the epicenter of America's war on booze during Prohibition. They just might be surprised how easily our local history could be incorporated into what they teach and how our children might understand their lessons far better if they understood that our nation's history happened in their own backyard.

—JAMES E. REAGEN

PROLOGUE

By 1921, the second year of America's Great Social Experiment, Northern New Yotk's communities, like the Ogdensburg, Massena, and Malone were discovering that Prohibition meant far more than just a few illegal speakeasies, some casual smuggling, and an occasional high-speed chase through the streets of downtown.

Violent confrontations, robberies, and gun battles during high-speed chases through the streets were becoming common as a more violent element of criminals began entering the illegal business. Rumors of gangs from New York City and other metropolitan areas taking control of the liquor business were circulating as illegal fortunes were being made, especially as some criminals discovered it was even more profitable to simply hijack liquor shipments from other smugglers or extort payments from those who had entered the business.

The result was a growing shadowy business empire that was spreading across the country as smugglers, bootleggers and speakeasy operators found themselves under increasing pressure from other criminal enterprises that demanded they pay part of their profits just for the right to stay in the increasingly profitable illegal business.

Meanwhile, the criminal justice authorities offered a patchwork approach to enforcement of what was increasingly becoming an unpopular law as the public's thirst for alcohol grew, encouraging many to turn a blind eye to the gin joints, blind pigs, speakeasies, and other criminal enterprises that were satisfying the demand for beer, wine, and liquor.

Some municipal police forces were fierce enforcers of the Prohibition laws. Others tended to focus on the rowdier lawbreakers as well as criminals from out of town who raced through their streets (to give the appearance of strict enforcement). In St. Lawrence County, the Sheriff's Department had initially ignored the new law, leaving it to the state and federal government to enforce its controversial prohibition, but as the problems worsened, the forces of Protestant temperance increasingly demanded action to clean up what many rural church-going folk saw as a problem associated with the waves of Catholic Irish, French-Canadian, Italian and Eastern Europeans who were moving into the North Country's major villages in search of industrial jobs at the turn of the century.

For St. Lawrence County communities like Ogdensburg, Massena, Potsdam, Canton and Gouverneur, Prohibition served as a divisive time with supporters on both sides, but a common view that gun battles, even those aimed at enforcing the law, were an unacceptable approach.

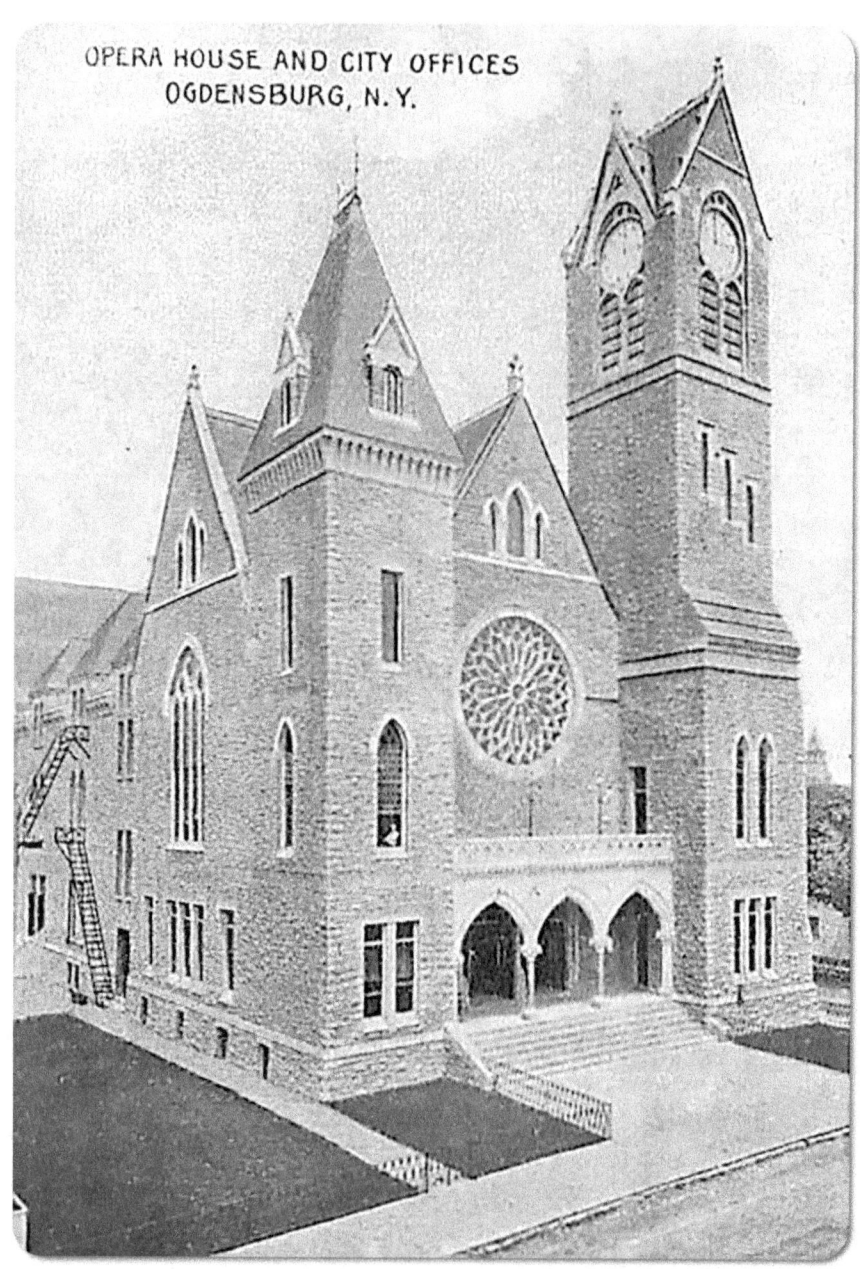

OGDENSBURG OLD OPERA HOUSE, POLICE STATION AND CITY AND TOWN OFFICES
PRESENT LOCATION OF CITY HALL (AUTHOR'S COLLECTION)

CHAPTER 1

MURDER ATTEMPT SHOCKS OGDENSBURG

When Charles "Brocky" Livingston staggered out of his taxi in front of the Ogdensburg Police Station at the Opera House at the corner of Ford and Caroline Streets, the young cab driver was covered in blood.[1]

With bullet wounds in his neck, arm and hip, Livingston told city police a harrowing tale of the murder attempt and his brush with death that Ogdensburg Advance and Weekly Democrat Editor George P. Darrow later described as "one of the most dastardly crimes in the annals of criminal history in the county."

Livingston described how a stranger with a British accent hired him to drive to the Red Mills area, where the English smuggler eventually shot the taximan three times after Livingston had fallen asleep waiting for a mysterious rendezvous in a brazen murder attempt.

The cabbie shakily told police that after he had been repeatedly shot, Livingston desperately wrestled with his attempted murderer in a life and death struggle that ended when the taxi driver overpowered his assailant and succeeded in taking the gun away from the man who had attempted to kill him.

---

[1] Ogdensburg Republican Journal, Oct. 23, 1921

With the tables turned, the gunman begged for his life before escaping from the badly wounded Ogdensburg man.

Livingston, a 25-year-old Ogdensburg cab driver, had served two years with the American army's expeditionary force in France during the "Great War," now known as World War 1.

Livingston told police that between 11 p.m. and 2 a.m. Saturday night, the stranger, who claimed his name was "Greenwich," appeared at his taxi stand and hired him to drive down the River Road (present day Rt. 37), saying he wanted to meet a man who was coming over from Canada in a small boat.

When they arrived near Red Mills, Livingston told police, the man, who was in the rear seat, told him to stop the car and wait for a mysterious man to arrive from across the river. Livingston says they waited quite a while and that he finally fell asleep.

He was suddenly awakened by a gunshot and felt a sharp pain in the back of his neck. He jumped up, and as he did so, another bullet struck him in the right arm. Livingston says when he realized his passenger was attempting to kill him, he dove through the window of his taxicab, but as he was making his desperate escape, the man in the rear seat fired again, hitting him in the left hip.

After striking the ground, Livingston told police he lay still, pretending he was dead. The British stranger got out of the cab and started to drag Livingston toward some bushes near the roadside. Although he was weak from loss of blood, and in a great deal of pain from his three gunshot wounds, Livingston waited for his chance and then grappled with his assailant for possession of the revolver.

After a vicious fight, he succeeded in overpowering and disarming his would-be killer.

Livingston admits he was tempted to shoot the man who tried to murder him, but he said the Englishman pleaded with him not to kill him, claiming he had a wife and two children.

What happened immediately afterwards, Livington did not make clear in his narrative on how the Canadian escaped, but the cab driver managed to stagger back to his car, and although extremely weak from his three bullet wounds and loss of blood, he managed to drive back to Ogdensburg at top speed until he reached the police station in the Opera House.

New York State Police Trooper H. K. Miller, Patrolman Charles Grenier and Alderman Charles S. Hubbard happened to be standing in front of city hall when the blood-soaked Livingston climbed out of his cab, stumbled toward them, and told his thrilling story.

The taxicab driver described his assailant as 5 feet 3 or 4 inches tall, 20-years-old, dark complexion, dark hair, wearing a long black overcoat with a fur collar and cap. Livingston says the man appeared to be a foreigner and that he was a total stranger to him.

The heavy caliber pistol which Livingston wrestled away from his assailant was turned over to the police.

The news concerning the attempted murder of the well-known city cab driver resulted in a team of law enforcement officers heading for Red Mills with a party of newspaper men trailing behind them.

After Livingston had been rushed to the hospital, Trooper Miller, Deputy Sheriff Edward McElligott, and Deputy Sheriff V. A. Wallace of Lisbon drove to Red Mills to the scene of the shooting where they found broken glass from Livingston's taxi window scattered about and blood stains on a camp road.

The officers fanned out in a search of the area to find Livingston's attacker.

The October 24, 1921, edition of the Ogdensburg Republican Journal reported the mysterious gunman had been captured.[2]

---

[2] Ogdensburg Republican Journal, Oct. 24, 1921

The headline reported:

LIVINGSTON'S ASSAILANT CAUGHT, THOMAS TURNER WANTED BY CANADIAN POLICE, CHARGED WITH SHOOTING TAXI DRIVER

Hires Him to Drive Down River Road Late At Night to Wait For Friend from Canada and Attacks Him as He Dozes In Seat, Tells Assistant District Attorney He Intended To Wound Livingston and Then Steal His Car, Officers Find Gunman Hiding Under Bed in Cottage Which He Had Broken Into; Defendant Held for the Grand Jury on Charge of Assault in First Degree; Victim in Hospital with Three Wounds but Will Recover.

The police investigation revealed the man who attempted to kill Brocky Livingston was no stranger to law enforcement on both sides of the international border.

Thomas Rowland Turner used aliases like "Jack Wilson" and "George Greenwood," during his criminal career before he made his murder attempt outside of Ogdensburg.

The 22-year-old Englishman fled Canada to avoid arrest as authorities closed in on him after he was linked to at least four crimes before his criminal career led him to Cape Vincent, Watertown and eventually to Ogdensburg where he attempted to kill Livingston.

Police arrested him after he was found hiding under a bed inside an empty cottage five miles below Ogdensburg near Camp Over-brook.

In a statement, Turner admitted to the shooting, but denied he was trying to murder the cabbie when he shot him three times. He claimed his real motive was to steal Livingston's car. Turner also denied rumors he wanted to steal Livingston's car to use it to haul smuggled liquor into the United States from Canada.

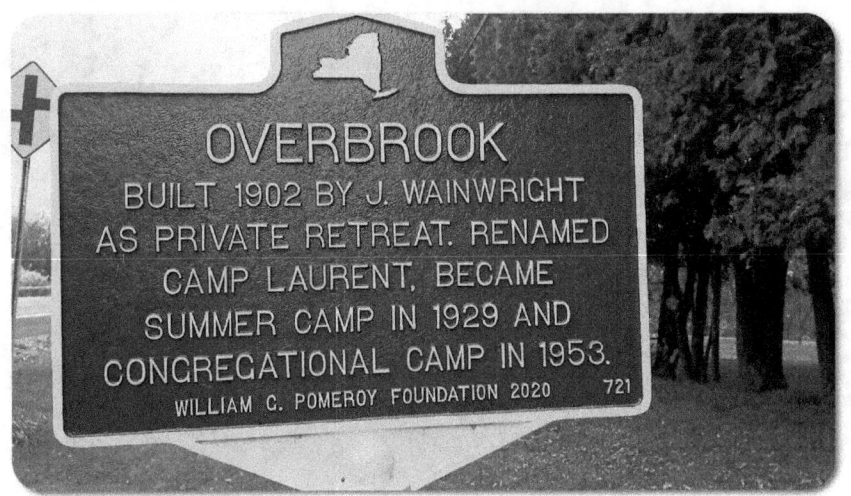

CAMP OVERBROOK IN RED MILLS AREA, NOT FAR FROM MURDER ATTEMPT
(AUTHOR'S COLLECTION)

The Assistant District Attorney stated Turner also denied he was part of an organized conspiracy to transport liquor across the St. Lawrence River from Canada, but he did not offer any explanation for why he was waiting for a boat to cross near Red Mills, what the boat may have contained or why it was coming to Lisbon's shore in the middle of the night.

U.S. Customs authorities and Immigration agents took an intense interest in the case, but authorities refused to say what might develop from the federal investigation or whether Turner had agreed to confidentially provide information on his American and Canadian confederates in exchange for reduced charges in the attempted murder case.

U.S. Customs Collector Henry Holland conferred behind closed doors with Assistant District Attorney Hanmer at city hall late in the afternoon and U.S. Immigration Inspectors Webber and Lane also were closeted with the prosecutor.

A. BARTON HEPBURN HOSPITAL (AUTHOR'S COLLECTION)

Shortly before 6 p.m., Turner was taken across the street to the office of Justice of the Peace Myron B. Gray and presented with a charge of assault in the first degree.

He pleaded not guilty and was remanded to the city jail without bail.

Livingston provided a more complete account of the events that led up to the shooting than the version he originally told witnesses when he first arrived at the Opera House, with three bullet wounds and weakened from the loss of blood.

Livingston, who collapsed after telling his initial story about his near-death experience, was taken to Hepburn Hospital where he was attended by Dr. John F. Free, hospital physician. State Trooper H. K. Miller, who was at the city police headquarters in the Opera House drove the wounded taxi man to the hospital and gave instructions to allow no one to see him until Assistant District Attorney Hammer of Massena, who was notified, arrived here. Mr. Hammer came here yesterday afternoon to investigate the affair. The attempted killer was captured by Deputy Sheriff McElligott, State Trooper Miller and

Police Officer Alfred Nicholson. Turner was discovered hiding under the bed in W. J. Carter's camp, five to eight miles downstream from Ogdensburg. Deputy Sheriff McElligott and a farmer lad who were searching the camps heard somebody moving about in the Carter cottage and McElligott summoned the other officers.

The place was surrounded, and the officers went inside and found Turner, who was unarmed and did not put up a fight. Turner broke into the camp by pulling out a screen door. He wore a blood-stained cap. When searched at headquarters, police found $269 in U.S. money (worth over $8,000 today), $2.50 in Canadian money, a blank check for a Canadian bank, a skeleton key and a few other articles in his pockets.

IN TOWN OF LISBON (PRESENT DAY) (AUTHOR'S COLLECTION)

When the police asked him, "Where is your gun," he replied. "The other fellow got it."

In the absence of St. Lawrence County District Attorney William Ingram of Ogdensburg, who had been called to Albany, his assistant, Andrew J. Hanmer of Massena, was called to Ogdensburg to help with the investigation. He questioned him in the council chamber. After securing Turner's statement, Mr. Hanmer went to Hepburn

Hospital and obtained a deposition from Livingston. The assistant district attorney then returned to city hall and asked Ogdensburg Police Chief John McCormick to summon two more witnesses, one of whom was Edward (Cubbie) Kiah, another taxi driver, who was in the room for a moment or two. A few minutes before Assistant District Attorney Hanmer returned to city hall, Immigration Inspectors Webber and Lane appeared. Webber said Turner had arrived at Ogdensburg on the ferry from Prescott, Ontario where he was wanted by the Canadian police.

U.S. Customs Collector Henry Holland came to police headquarters shortly after Assistant District Attorney Hanmer arrived back from the hospital and the entire party with Chief of Police McCormick retired to the council chamber and closed the door.

Half an hour later, Assistant District Attorney Hammer came out of the room and told reporters he would give a statement. Before he started to tell what happened, Collector Holland whispered to Mr. Hanmer asking him not to give out certain information. Mr. Hanmer nodded his head and said he would not. The Assistant District Attorney told the reporters that the federal authorities were "checking" up on the stories told by the witnesses. Assistant District Attorney Hanmer explained: "The right name of the defendant is Thomas Turner, alias "Jack Wilson," and alias "George Greenwood." Turner is the son of George and Nellie Turner, of the Queens Hotel, Halifax, England.

"He served in the Canadian army and later went home and then came to Canada four months ago. He is alleged to have committed three or four crimes in Canada, among them stealing and forgery. He came from Kingston, Ontario to Cape Vincent and then went to Watertown a week ago where he joined an illegal bootlegging and smuggling operation.

CUBBY'S TAXI STAND (OGDENSBURG LIBRARY)

"Saturday morning, he came to Ogdensburg in a car with John Fitzgerald of Alexandria Bay and two other men from Watertown, one called Clinton. They came here to put together a deal for whiskey with a man in Ogdensburg whose name is withheld for the present.

Saturday night, soon after the first show, or about 9:20 p.m., Turner walked across the street and approached Livingston, and Eddie "Cubbie" Kiah, who were sitting on the bumper of Kiah's car.

Livingston asked him if he wanted a car. Turner asked if that was Livingston's car and Livingston said no but that he had one just like it. Livingston and Turner then walked over to the other car and Turner asked him what his charges were, and he said 20 cents a mile. Prior to going to the hack stand, Turner came from Marian Fraser's residence.

They started out and went eight or nine miles down the River Road. Turner told Livingston to stop as he wanted to wait for a fellow.

Turner says they turned the car to the side of the road, shut off the lights and waited about an hour.

Turner finally said he guessed the other fellow would not show up and they would drive back to Fraser's in the city. The prosecutor expressed the opinion that Turner intended to shoot Livingston while they were waiting in the cab, but the gunman lost his nerve.

FORD STREET, LOOKING WEST, OGDENSBURG, N. Y.

HOTEL NORMAN ON LEFT (AUTHOR'S COLLECTION)

"They returned to Fraser's house. Turner got out and went to the door. Fraser drove into the yard and Turner got into his car and talked with him for a few minutes. Fraser says Turner wanted him to cash a check which he refused to do.

Livingston drove him to the Hotel Norman. After going inside briefly, Turner said they would go back to Red Mills as the fellow he expected to meet might be there by then. Livingston protested, saying he did not care to go and asked Turner to pay him his mileage. Turner said, "stick by me and help me finish this job and I'll give you $25.' (Approximately $428 today). They went back to the same place down the river road and stopped and turned out the lights and waited there for some time. It was raining and Livingston said he began to doze. Turner was in the back seat.

"Suddenly, Livingston was aroused by a pinch in the neck. He jumped up and something hit him on the arm. He then realized that he was being shot at and he jumped out through the window of the car.

As he was going out, the other fellow shot him in the hip. The gunman repeatedly claimed he did not intend to kill Livingston. He only intended to shoot and wound him, steal the car, and go.

Livingston says that when he dove out of the car's window, he laid on the ground motionless, pretending he was dead. Turner thought he had killed the taxi driver and started to drag him into the bushes to hide the body. At a favorable moment, Livingston grabbed Turner's hand and wrestled the gun away from him. Livingston said he was getting weaker, and he feared the fellow might take the gun from him and finish the job.

RED MILLS IN LISBON (AUTHOR'S COLLECTION)

Once Livingston wrestled the gun away from his would-be murderer, Turner begged him not to take his life, claiming he had a wife and children.

Pointing the gun at Turner, Livingston ordered him to go on up the road. Turner obeyed, going up the road and out of sight, hiding in the woods until daylight. Next morning, Turner broke into the Carter cottage. He pulled open the screen door and crawled in. The officers later found him inside, hiding under the bed.

Turner told police that when he and his companions came here from Watertown to begin their smuggling efforts, they found the river too rough that day to negotiate a passage. The other fellow left him. Turner decided to begin his own smuggling enterprise, but he knew he needed a car. The Assistant District Attorney said Turner impressed him as being "a tough Englishman." Mr. Hanmer also stated that as far as he had ascertained, Turner and Livingston had never seen each other before the murder attempt.

SHERIFF FISHBECK HERE

St. Lawrence County Sheriff Lawrence A. Fishbeck was called to Ogdensburg to assist the local authorities in their search for the gunman. The Sheriff returned to the county seat after the arrest had been made.

The Advance and Weekly Democrat newspaper reported Livingston was recovering from his multiple gunshot wounds and was expected to be released from the hospital within a week.[3]

The Advance reported Turner "had a bad reputation in Canada where he is wanted for several crimes. Canadian authorities told Ogdensburg investigators that shortly after arriving in Montreal after returning to England after the war, he got mixed up in criminal activ-

---

[3] Ogdensburg Advance and Weekly Democrat, Oct. 25, 1921

ities and liquor smuggling. The newspaper also filled in some of the blanks surrounding the shooting and the Englishman accused in the brutal crime.

The newspaper reported Turner's father gave his son $1,000 to establish himself in a business in Montreal, Canada after the war, but the young man soon got mixed up with bootleggers and an illicit smuggling operation that led to the loss of all the money his father had given him. The Ogdensburg Advance also raised questions whether Turner served in the Army during the war in Europe.

But most of all, George Darrow, the editor of the Ogdensburg Advance and Weekly Democrat questioned whether the real story of all the events surrounding the brutal murder attempt had been shared with the public.

"It is thought that the full story of the shooting has not yet been told," the newspaper suggested, arguing "that later developments may result in nabbing the head of the 'whiskey ring' who the newspaper suggested "may be a prominent businessperson of this city."

"The story told by Livingston and Turner varies," Darrow pointed out. "Livingston makes no mention of the second trip down the river."

The visits to the Hotel Norman and other locations had not been fully explained, Darrow argued, raising questions whether there was more to the mysterious circumstances surrounding the shooting than either of the two men had offered in their statements to police.

Who were they meeting in Red Mills?

What was the real purpose of the meeting?

Who did they meet with at the Hotel Norman?

Was it true that they had never met each other before the evening of their fateful trip to Red Mills?

Had police and federal investigators really reported everything they had learned from their investigation?

Or might either of the two men have told more to police and federal authorities that might lead to other arrests?

Was there a mysterious criminal underworld leader of the "whiskey ring" in Ogdensburg?

CARTHAGE EXCHANGE BANK (AUTHOR'S COLLECTION)

The Advance's editor raised these questions but offered little in the way of answers. While the Ogdensburg Advance and Weekly Democrat speculated whether the story of the shooting was just the tip of a much larger criminal iceberg connected to illegal liquor smuggling in the Ogdensburg area, the Oct. 25th edition of the Ogdensburg Republican Journal was focusing on Turner's troubles with Canada's law enforcement agencies before his arrival in Ogdensburg.[4]

The Republican Journal's headline reported:

---

[4] Ogdensburg Republican Journal, Oct. 25, 1921

Canadian Officers Seek Goods Stolen by Turner in Prescott, Sold Watch, Ring to Watertown Man and Left Bag There

County Constable H. W. Jackson of Prescott, Ontario, William Barton, a retired banker, and Prescott Chief of Police Dunn were in the city yesterday interviewing Ogdensburg Chief of Police John McCormick in relation to the case of Thomas Turner, the young Englishman who shot Charles Livingston, taxi man, early Saturday morning at Red Mills. Turner is wanted in Prescott for stealing a watch, some rings and even a quantity of underwear belonging to Barton.

Constable Jackson, who was formerly chief of police at Prescott, has been working on the case for some time and suspected Turner of being the guilty party. Jackson interviewed Turner and learned that he had sold the watch and ring to a man in Watertown and had left a club bag containing the other stolen articles in the check room of the railroad station in Watertown.

Turner told the Prescott investigators he thought he left the check in the Carter cottage down the river where he was arrested Sunday morning.

With W. J. Carter, the owner of the cottage, the officers went to the Lisbon camp and "found the baggage check, also a bank book issued by the National Exchange Bank of Carthage to Turner under the name of George Greenwood."

Turner admitted to the Prescott authorities he opened an account in the Carthage bank by depositing the sum of $16. His checkbook showed the stub of a check for $15 which he had drawn October 21st in favor of R. Parker of Carthage in payment for his gun.

A U.S Immigration head tax receipt issued to Turner under the name of Jackson Wilson when he entered the country at Cape Vincent also was found.

The Canadian officers told the Ogdensburg police that Turner had not actually served in the army as he claimed but had been in the radio service during the war.

The Canadians also reported that when Turner returned home to England after the war his father set him up in business, but the venture turned out badly and he came to America last June.

The Journal reported that Brocky Livingston was not recovering as quickly from his bullet wounds as had been believed initially.

His father, John Livingston, a well-known tinsmith of the city, told the newspaper that if his son died from his injuries, Turner would face charges of murder in the first degree and that investigators had told him his conviction would be a foregone conclusion as he had admitted in his statement to Assistant District Attorney Hanmer that he shot the "taxi man, intending to wound him and make off with his car."

The Oct. 27, 1921, edition of the Ogdensburg Republican Journal reported that investigators lost no time in following up on the information they had received in relation to Turner's Prescott burglary.[5]

The newspaper reported:

Prescott Banker's Valuables Located in Watertown.

Every article of jewelry and other items which were stolen from the residence of William Barton, a retired banker of Prescott, Ont., by Thomas Turner, who is at the county jail at Canton for the shooting of Charles Livingston, a taxicab driver of this city last Saturday, was recovered in Watertown late Tuesday afternoon.

Detective Captain A. S. Wood, assisting Constable H. W. Jackson of Prescott, accompanied by Mr. Barton, went to

---

[5] Ogdensburg, Republican Journal, Oct. 27, 1921

Watertown early Tuesday afternoon by automobile from here. They returned early Tuesday night.

WATERTOWN RAILROAD DEPOT (AUTHOR'S COLLECTION)

Most of the stolen property was found in a club bag which had been checked at the New York Central Railroad station baggage room there a few weeks ago.

Constable Jackson took the check with him to Watertown. In the club bag were various articles of highly valued jewelry and clothing. A diamond ring, valued at $100, and an open face watch, valued at $25, which were stolen from the Barton residence, were recovered by Detective Captain Wood.

Constable Jackson was informed by Turner in this city on Monday of the whereabouts of the two pieces of jewelry. The ring and watch "were found in a secondhand shop in Watertown. All the stolen property has been recovered except for seven ounces of pure gold (worth $140 in 1921, worth $16,000 today). Turner claimed to the constable that it was in the bag, but it was not found there.

While the shooting of Livingston had raised a host of questions and speculation that it might lead to even more important revelations about Ogdensburg's criminal underworld, news reports concerning the case failed to answer any of the tantalizing questions that the Advance had raised.

Less than four months later, news coverage of the sensational shooting ended with a less than exciting conclusion when the Canadian gunman was quietly allowed by law enforcement and prosecutors to cop a generous plea bargain in St. Lawrence County Court.

The Feb. 23, 1922, edition of the Ogdensburg Republican Journal reported the anticlimactic end to the story:

> Thomas Turner, who was charged with assaulting Charles Livingston, a local taxi driver, at a lonely spot on the River Road several months ago, firing several shots at him, three of which hit him, was given not less than four years nor more than eight years in state prison. Livingston narrowly escaped with his life in this fracas, being assaulted while asleep in his car. Turner was represented by Attorney Leo J. Crary of Canton.

The newspaper reports never showed whether the mysterious Turner had ever provided information to police about who he was supposed to meet on the shore in Red Mills the night of the shooting and whether there was more to the murder attempt on Livingston than just a simple car theft.

Or why investigators and prosecutors agreed to such a short prison sentence for such a serious crime as shooting someone in the commission of an armed robbery.

Or why Livingston was chosen by Turner when the Englishman could have more easily chosen Edward "Cubby" Kiah whose cab was right there on Ford Street when Turner approached the two taxi drivers.

Was it just a vehicle theft that went wrong?

Or had Turner come to Ogdensburg specifically intending to kill Livingston for some undisclosed reason?

WINDMILL ON CANADIAN SIDE OF RIVER ACROSS FROM OGDENSBURG, N.Y.
(AUTHOR'S COLLECTION)

CHAPTER 2

RIVER SMUGGLING TRIP ENDS IN DROWNING

OGDENSBURG - When Stanley Montgomery slipped beneath the waves of the St. Lawrence River on a frozen January night in 1921, the bootlegger's death was dismissed as just another foolish smuggler who underestimated how dangerous a winter passage could be rowing between Prescott, Ontario and Ogdensburg, New York.[6]

His wife, however, just could not believe it.

Her husband, Stanley, was no fool.

The 40-year-old truck driver had served his country as a member of Company D which had gathered at the Ford Street Armory for years to train to defend his nation.

The idea that he had accidentally tipped over his rowboat and lost his grip while waiting for help just did not ring true to the mother of his children.

Yes, she told authorities, she knew her husband had been smuggling booze illegally into the country.

But she wanted to know what had happened to the $2,000 he had told her he was carrying with him during his trip across the river.

---

[6] Ogdensburg Advance and Weekly Democrat, Jan. 6, 1921

Why had the other smugglers left her husband behind while they rowed for shore and safety?

Was he murdered by his criminal associates for the $2,000 his wife claimed he possessed when he slipped under the waves of the frozen St. Lawrence River?

And was there any connection to the mysterious death of R. Harry Moore who had also died in a strange drowning off Ogdensburg's shore at the same time?

Authorities said they never found any hard proof to back up his wife's suspicions.

But Mrs. Montgomery put up a reward in both Ogdensburg and Prescott to try to find out whether anyone had information that could shed light on the mysterious death of her husband.

Stanley Montgomery and Tommy Moore had built a successful, if illegal, enterprise smuggling booze across the St. Lawrence River from Prescott to Ogdensburg. By January 4th of 1921, they were making enough money that they believed a little ice on the river between the two border communities need not prevent them from continuing to make money from their growing smuggling business.

Montgomery was rowing across from Prescott's historic Windmill when his boat capsized with Moore in it.

The two men called for help as they struggled in the freezing waters off Windmill Point, downstream from Prescott.

Montgomery drowned before help arrived.

His business partner, Moore, a Fourth Ward resident, initially claimed they had been duck hunting when the mishap occurred.

Canton's Commercial Advertiser reported in its Jan. 11th, 1921, edition that one of the men had fired shots which attracted the attention of Alva Frasier of Prescott who managed to rescue Moore.[7]

---

[7] Canton Commercial Advertiser, Jan. 11, 1921

Moore managed to pull himself to the edge of the overturned green punt. When he fell off the boat and struggled back to the surface, Frasier grasped him by the hair and pulled him into his boat.

"He was taken to the farmhouse of William Murdock on the Canadian side below Prescott, where he was attended by Dr. McPherson. Moore was given stimulants, and sometime later revived sufficiently to give his name and that of his companion who had disappeared. That was all he was able to tell. The theory was that the accident occurred when the men were changing seats. Frasier saw nothing of Montgomery, and it is supposed that he became exhausted and went down."

Initially, reports circulated through Ogdensburg that the man rescued was R. Harry Moore who was also believed to have drowned off the Rutland Railroad dock.

Prescott Police Chief Jackson said that his investigation concluded that two separate, unrelated, drownings had occurred that had created confusion because both involved men named Moore.

Thomas Moore was said to be a son of Patrick Moore, a resident of the Fourth Ward, and about 25 years of age. Montgomery was a son of the late Ransom Montgomery and was about 40 years old. He was formerly a member of Company D and lately had been employed as a motor truck driver.

His wife was notified of the accident and late last night crossed to Prescott to go to the farmhouse where Moore was being cared for.

An investigation into the death by District Attorney W. D. Ingram found no evidence of foul play.

The District Attorney attributed the death to the two men capsizing the boat because they got drunk and shifted positions in the rough waters of the St. Lawrence, capsizing it in the freezing January waters.

Potsdam's Courier Freeman reported in its Jan. 12, 1921, edition that the two had crossed on Monday night, secured the liquor and were ready to return Tuesday, but decided to wait until dark because they feared they would be discovered by authorities. They remained at the farmhouse of a Canadian that day and set out on the ill-fated trip.[8]

Moore said that after the boat had nearly reached deep water it struck a piece of ice, puncturing the craft.

The two men attempted to row furiously across the river despite the freezing water rushing into the craft from the hole.

When the water had risen to more than eight inches, the two decided to intentionally tip the boat over and to cling to it because they feared it might sink with them in it.

Montgomery hung on to the boat as long as he could but in the freezing water, he became exhausted, lost hope of rescue and lost his grip.

"Moore sought to reach him and hold him above the surface, but his efforts were in vain. Montgomery had fired four shots to attract attention to their desperate plight but slipped beneath the water before help arrived.

Rumors circulating in Ogdensburg were that Montgomery had $2,000 in his pocket when he went under.

The Jan. 13th edition of the Advance and Weekly Democrat reported that there may have been two other boats loaded with liquor "but with characteristic bootlegger sympathy they abandoned their comrades" to their fates in the frozen waters of the St. Lawrence.[9]

The Advance also pointed out the drowned smuggler was carrying a pistol and "prepared to do murder" if anyone attempted to interfere with his illegal expedition. The other mysterious drowning

---

[8] Potsdam Courier Freeman, Jan. 12, 1921
[9] Ogdensburg Advance and Weekly St. Lawrence Democrat, Jan. 13

that happened the same day involved R. Harry Moore, aged 34, an electrical inspector in the employment of the New York Association of "Underwriters," with headquarters in Watertown. Investigators believed he accidentally drowned off the dock near the Rutland railroad depot about 8 o'clock the morning of the Montgomery drowning.

PASSENGER TRAIN CAR PARKED AT THE NEW YORK CENTRAL TRAIN DEPOT. OGDENSBURG FEATURED TWO RAILROAD DEPOTS, THE RUTLAND AT THE PRESENT-DAY PORT OF OGDENSBURG AND THE NEW YORK CENTRAL WHERE THE PRESENT DAY FREIGHTHOUSE RESTAURANT IS LOCATED.

A cloth hat containing his name was found on the dock near a hole in the ice. In the railway station at the Rutland Railroad port were found two bags with tags attached bearing Mr. Moore's name. The hat was found on the dock by Samuel Pelkey, who notified the railroad officials, and they in turn informed the police.

Ogdensburg Police Sergeant John McDonal visited the scene and found footprints on the frost covered planks leading to the edge of the dock. One of the planks was about six feet in length and fastened in the middle with a spike in such a manner that if a person stepped on the outer end, he would cause it to tilt toward the water and cause someone on it to fall.

Investigators believe that Moore, after leaving his hand-baggage in the station, strolled along the dock to wait until the train was due to leave but stepped on the loose plank and fell into the freezing water after striking his head as he fell.

"No cries for help were heard by anyone in the vicinity. As soon as Moore's relatives were notified of the affair, they arranged to have the river dragged and while this operation was continued until dark no trace of the body was discovered. Mr. Moore left his home on Patterson Street yesterday morning, telling his wife that he was going to Canton on a business trip and would probably go out on the bus. J. F. Bryant, the ticket agent at the Rutland station, stated that a man called at the window about 8 a.m., and asked when the next train would leave. Bryant replied at 9:10. Mr. Bryant was busy making out a report at the time and the man left the window before he looked up, so the agent did not see him. This is now supposed to have been Moore. The hat found on the dock was turned over to the police and later given to relatives of Mr. Moore, along with his two bags which were found in the station. The police expressed the opinion that the drowning of Moore was purely accidental.

Mr. Moore was well known in this city, having been employed by Ogdensburg Power and Light Co., as superintendent of its electrical department for three years before he resigned to enter the service of the Underwriters' association. He traveled out of Watertown and his territory included the northern counties.

Moore was born in Lisbon. His wife is the sister of William H. Green, and they have two children. He also has two brothers, James D. Moore of Lisbon, and Wade Moore of Ogdensburg.

While the Moore drowning investigation led to a conclusion that it was just an unfortunate accident, the investigation into the bootlegger's drowning on Jan. 4 led to federal indictments against three men - taxicab driver Bernard J. Steinberg, Ernest Walker, and Thomas Moore. Stanley Montgomery, who had died on the ill-fated trip, was also indicted.

Steinberg and Walker were indicted for conspiracy in connection with the smuggling ring.

Mrs. Montgomery told investigators she believed her husband had been murdered, pointing out that he was carrying a considerable sum of money at the time of his alleged drowning.

City Police and the District Attorney said their investigation found no evidence of foul play.

Unconvinced, Mrs. Montgomery posted a reward on both sides of the St. Lawrence for anyone who could help her family retrieve her husband's body or had information related to his death.

Horse And Sleigh In 1920s Provided A Way to Haul Supplies in Winter Months

CHAPTER 3

MURDER, ROBBERY PLAGUE BORDER

CHAMPLAIN, Jan. 13 – When Joseph Senecal saw two masked gunmen stepping out of the bushes into the path of his horse drawn sleigh as he approached the Canadian border from the Quebec side, he immediately knew what they were after.[10]

The hijackers wanted the load of liquor he was bringing to Champlain, New York to make some quick money to support his family.

A resident of Hemmingford, Que., Senecal was hauling several cases of illegal booze on his sleigh. He was hurrying along through the early morning light when the two hold-up men stepped into the highway and ordered him to halt.

Instead of stopping, Senecal whipped up his team of horses to outrun the bandits, but the hijackers managed to jump into the sleigh and grappled with him.

During the struggle, one of the criminals fired the contents of his revolver into Senecal's body. Senecal later was taken to the Champlain Valley hospital in Plattsburgh where he died of his wounds.

In the winter of 1921, Hemmingford was a dry Canadian town

---

[10] Ogdensburg Republican Journal, Jan. 13, 1921

just across the border from Champlain, New York on the highway between the village and Montreal.

When a critically injured Senecal rolled off his sleigh into the road, the highwaymen, afraid the gunshots might draw unwanted attention to their hijacking, ran away without taking the liquor.

A mortally wounded Senecal was found by a resident of Hemmingford and transported 12 miles to Champlain where an ambulance from the Champlain Valley hospital in Plattsburgh was called.

He was unconscious when he arrived at the hospital

Clinton County Sheriff Coffey and a posse with United States Marshal Murray and a squad of U.S. Customs officers began a search, scouring the country for the bandits who they believed were from the American side of the border.

The Canadian officials also searched the area to determine if they could find evidence that might indicate where the murderers came from and who they are.

Unfortunately, the mysterious murder only showed that bootleggers and smugglers along the border were growing more brazen.

In some cases, the robberies were simple hijackings being conducted by thieves who found they could avoid putting up any money to buy a shipment of liquor by just holding up the smugglers who were purchasing liquor in Canada and smuggling it across the border. Criminals who hijacked loads from bootleggers faced serious risks during the booze robberies since many were heavily armed to protect themselves and their illicit goods.

But the holdups offered a distinct advantage to robbers who were willing to take the risk of holding up other criminals.

Once the robbery was over, the victims could not go to the police to report the theft of their cargo of liquor.

That is also why investigators believed some of the thefts were part of an organized effort by hoodlums connected with organized crime outfits who were attempting to monopolize the smuggling efforts, demanding that other criminals pay them a percentage of the value of their shipment or face violent and sometimes deadly consequences.

Unfortunately, for the organized crime elements that were attempting to take control of the smuggling and illegal booze industry that was popping up along both sides of the border, the hoodlums were finding it just as difficult to catch those who wanted to avoid paying them off as the law enforcement agencies that were trying to shut the illegal trade off.

For the federal, state, and local law enforcement community, it was often difficult to determine whether shootings were the work of freelancers out to make a quick buck or the growing organized crime groups that were attempting to take control of the border.

WATERTOWN OPERA HOUSE (AVON THEATER) (AUTHOR'S COLLECTION)

TWO PRESCOTT CITIZENS FINED FOR BOOTLEGGING; WOMAN AND BROTHER CHARGED WITH TRANSPORTING LIQUOR

UTICA, Jan. 13. —When Caroline McAsken and her brother, James Sweeney, of Prescott pulled up in front of the Avon Theater in Watertown, a city police officer on the lookout for a stolen car pulled them over because they seemed suspicious.

Their vehicle was riding suspiciously low to the ground.[11]

When he searched their car, he arrested them for hauling 90 bottles of liquor.

Their attorney, Nathaniel M. Smith of Watertown, asked for mercy from the federal court, arguing that the pair were hauling the liquor from Malone through Watertown because McAsken's husband, George, had been a cripple for seven years and the family needed money for hospital expenses. The attorney produced sworn statements from Prescott Ontario's Mayor and the Canadian port city's Customs Collector attesting to their good character and several physicians who verified her husband's medical issues.

U.S. Federal Judge Cooper questioned her at great length. She said that lacking money to care for her husband, who was in a hospital, she decided to secure the liquor from a farmer named Leblanc near Malone and that she got her brother to drive the automobile.

She was fined $100, and her brother was fined $75. They lost their car.

---

[11] Republican Journal, Jan. 14, 1921

MASSENA MAN SURPRISED! NO HONOR AMONG CRIMINALS

MASSENA - When Frank Kuras of Massena bought a load of illegal liquor from the Bronchetti brothers, he thought he was dealing with honorable men.

But when James, Joseph and Nicholas Bronchetti stole the 10 cases of liquor from him that he had paid $460 to obtain, he confronted them, and they grudgingly agreed to return it.[12]

Later, when they refused, keeping the money and the liquor, Kuras decided they had left him with no choice. If they had no sense of honor and their words were no good, he would do what he needed to do to obtain justice.

They had swindled him out of $460 (worth $7,200 today).

With the average working person earning about $60 a week, if he was lucky, the Bronchetti brothers had ripped him off to the tune of almost eight weeks of pay!

With nowhere else to turn, Kuras sought the help of the courts, bringing charges against the brothers, asking the District Attorney to investigate.

The St. Lawrence County Grand Jury listened to his story of the woes caused by the deceitful Bronchetti brothers who had taken advantage of him.

After listening carefully to his testimony, the grand jurors voted to indict the Bronchetti brothers.

They were held on $3,000 bond. Their father, Michael, paid the bond for their release. After news reports publicized the dangers of doing business with Massena's Bronchetti family, the family agreed to make restitution.

---

[12] Massena Observer, Jan. 6, 1921

FEDERAL G MEN ARRIVE IN MALONE TO STOP SMUGGLING

MALONE - Four federal prohibition agents have arrived in Malone to assist Federal Agent John R. Kennedy in the enforcement of the Volstead act along the Franklin County section of the Canadian border. [13]

The agents have been assigned to assist local, state, and federal authorities because of the "persistent rumors" of liquor smuggling in that vicinity.

"An active campaign against the illicit traffic" will be started at once under the direction of Agent Kennedy.

Three federal agents from Detroit, Michigan - L. Marks, W. Golden, and R. Jacobson - will join John Dempsey of New York City on the border crackdown.

2 POTSDAM MEN TEAM UP WITH UTICA'S ITALIANS ON BOOZE SMUGGLING, 100 CASES OF WHISKEY, GIN, SIX PERSONS HELD

POTSDAM, Oct. 20 - One of the biggest liquor seizures ever made (as of 1921) was pulled off here about 4 this morning when a group of Italian gangsters from Utica and two Potsdam men were arrested by federal prohibition agents, customs officers and Franklin County sheriff's men who seized two truckloads and one automobile containing 100 cases of whiskey, gin and high wines, valued at more than $5,000 (worth $80,000 today).[14]

The trucks were stopped a few miles outside of Potsdam on the Hopkinton Road and the Dodge touring car was seized in the heart of the residential section in Potsdam on Elm Street, concluding a

---

[13] Ogdensburg Republican Journal, Jan. 12, 1921

[14] Republican Journal, Oct. 21, 1921

high-speed chase after the Potsdam men fled, leaving their Utica colleagues behind.

The two Potsdam men were in the touring car. They gave their names as Earl Brownell and John Regan, residing in Potsdam and vicinity.

Brownell got away temporarily; but Regan was held.

Five Italians were with the trucks, all from Utica. The whole outfit was taken to Malone immediately following the seizure, where arraignment will be made before the United States Commissioner.

CONFISCATED DISTILLERY (PUBLIC DOMAIN)

CHAPTER 4

OGDENSBURG'S FIRST MOONSHINE DISTILLERY SEIZED ON OAK STREET

William Brenno of Oak Street earned the distinction of owning the first moonshine still seized in Ogdensburg by federal agents after Prohibition.

While most Ogdensburg bootleggers hauled liquor and beer across the St. Lawrence River from Canada, a few enterprising businessmen, like Brenno, decided to produce their own locally made 200 proof "white lightning."

After Prohibition Agents were able to obtain proof that the Westside man was producing moonshine for his thirsty Second Ward neighborhood, the feds decided to launch a raid to put the illegal distillery out of business.

When officers arrived at Brenno's Pine Street home, the officers found the house locked.

The officers obtained a search warrant for the Brenno premises from U.S. Commissioner Myron Gray after Agent Dillon presented proof of the illegal alcohol making operation.

They left one officer on guard while the others went back downtown to the U.S. Post Office and Federal Courthouse on State Street to get the search warrant.

JAMES E. REAGEN

While they went to get their search warrant, Brenno and another
man who was also in the house, escaped out a window.

MASSENA TRIO PAY FINE, LOSE CAR & WHISKEY AFTER TRIP

UTICA, Jan. 16. - Frank Ryan, Eddie Ryan, and William Quinn
of Massena learned the hard way that smuggling booze could be
an expensive proposition when they lost their vehicle, liquor and
received expensive fines for their troubles.[15]

Federal Judge Frank Cooper fined Eddie $50 and his brother
Frank and their friend Quinn $200 each for their failed business ven-
ture.

Frank Ryan had suffered the loss of a leg and an arm in a work-
place accident. He decided to supplement his $4.25 a day pension
by withdrawing $870 from the bank and hiring Quinn to take him
and his mentally disabled brother, Eddie, to Canada to purchase
liquor.

They went first to Fort Covington and made inquiries about purchasing whiskey but decided that the people who offered to help
them were too unsavory to trust.

"We were afraid they'd double-cross us," explained Frank to the
court, "so we went on to Canada and inquired of a farmer near St.
Angeles about getting some liquor."

The farmer telephoned a neighbor who supplied them with 12
cases of whiskey for $590

When they were caught, their Hudson car, which they had purchased in Watertown, was confiscated.

---

[15] Ogdensburg Republican Journal, Jan. 17, 1921

ALEXANDRIA BAY YACHT OWNER'S LIQUOR SUPPLY STOLEN

ALEXANDRIA BAY, Feb. 10.—A reward of $50 for information leading to the arrest of thieves who robbed the yacht Kismet of 100 bottles of liquor valued at $1,000 (worth $15,000 today) has been offered by Capt. Abner E. Wagoner, caretaker of the yacht.[16]

Yet no clue, except the tools with which the cracksmen worked and the tracks of the auto which carried away the booty, have been found.

The district attorney's office was notified, and a wire was sent to Commodore W. H. Downey, owner of the yacht, now in the Bermudas, regarding the theft.

It developed today that the boat had been stocked with liquor in the spring of 1917. It was sent here for storage on the boat, the owner realizing that transportation of liquor would eventually become difficult with the 18th Amendment prohibiting the sale, manufacture, or transportation of alcohol. Commodore Downey, whose home is at Tenafly, N. J., insisted to investigators that he does not drink, nor have his guests had occasion to use the liquor except on rare occasions. Some were used for cooking purposes, but since 1917 only a dozen bottles were consumed.

---

[16] Ogdensburg Republican Journal, Jan. 21, 1921

MAPLE CITY SCANDAL-THE OGDENSBURG REPUBLICAN JOURNAL'S FRONT-PAGE HEADLINE OF FEB. 10TH, 1921, TOLD THE STORY (TOP HEADLINE, RIGHT HAND NEWS COLUMN). OGDENSBURG'S POLICE HAD BEEN "ASSAULTED BY GANGSTERS" AND DRIVEN FROM A SECOND WARD SPEAKEASY DURING A RAID ON A NOTORIOUS WESTSIDE POOL ROOM ON NEW YORK AVENUE.

CHAPTER 5

BRENNO GANG BEATS UP POLICE AT RED DEVIL POOL HALL

When Ogdensburg Police Chief John McCormick personally led a raid into the city's notorious West Side speakeasy, known in the Second Ward neighborhood as the "Red Devil Pool Hall," he did not reckon with the Brenno gang.[17]

A little over a century ago, in 1921, Ogdensburg discovered the dramatic rise in lawlessness caused by Prohibition, liquor smuggling and illegal drinking establishments had led to what the Maple City's newspapers described as "a wave of lawlessness" in some city neighborhoods.

Criminal gangs were even breaking into the homes of other smugglers and bootleggers to hijack their supplies of illegal booze to corner the illicit market.

Law abiding citizens were angry at these brazen thefts and fearful that the break-ins might not be limited to just other criminals. If the criminals could get away with robbing each other, wasn't it likely that honest homeowners might be next?

In 1921, the difficulties facing Ogdensburg's small police depart-

---

[17] The Republican Journal, Ogdensburg, Feb. 10, 1921

ment came to a very public and embarrassing crisis point after officers suffered a humiliating defeat at the hands of what Ogdensburg's
three local newspapers - (the Republican Journal, The Advance and
St. Lawrence Weekly Democrat, and the Ogdensburg News) called
the "Brenno gang" during a raid on a notorious Second Ward speakeasy.

Known as the "Red Devil Pool Hall," (Advance News, September
7, 1975) located at the corner of New York Avenue and Pine Street,
inside Paul Cousineau's neighborhood store, the watering hole was a
favorite gathering place for the "Brenno gang," which was described
in the Feb. 16, 1921 edition of the Republican Journal as being "a
band of men who are alleged to have committed a series of depredations on the city's West Side during the past few months." [18]

While most of Ogdensburg's extensive Brenno family were considered solid citizens, one small branch of the Brennos was considered in some quarters as a notorious band of bootleggers, smugglers,
and street toughs.[19]

The leader of the Second Ward's most famous band of outlaws
in the 1920s was James "Jimmy" Brenno, whose Pine Street family
were no strangers to Ogdensburg's law enforcement community and
criminal justice administrators.

The Brennos and their fellow regulars who frequented what they
fondly called the "Red Devil Pool Hall" on New York Avenue had
earned a reputation for not being afraid to deliver their own brand of
Second Ward Street justice to those who earned their wrath.

On a cold February night, Ogdensburg Police Chief John D.
McCormick, Sgt. John J. McDonal and Officer Frank Beach discovered the Brenno gang posed unique challenges to a poorly trained

---

[18] Advance News, Sept. 7, 1975 (Interview with Jimmy Brenno 50 years after the
incident)

[19] Ogdensburg Republican Journal, Feb. 16, 1921

and aging police force, especially as the Prohibition era turned increasingly violent, offering easy money to anyone tempted to walk the shady side of the Maple City's streets.

THE WEST SIDE OF OGDENSBURG IN 1876 (AUTHOR'S COLLECTION)

The ensuing city-wide scandal caused a major uproar that forced Ogdensburg to examine its approach to community policing in a time when respect for law enforcement was being increasingly tested as growing numbers of citizens were ignoring the newly enacted constitutional amendment and resulting state and local laws banning the sale, manufacture, importation and transportation of liquor to an increasingly thirsty populace.

For law enforcement officers, including Ogdensburg's own police department, it was a challenging time to wear a badge when even law-abiding citizens were turning to criminals to provide them with beer, wine, liquor and sometimes, "shady" places where they could relax with their "refreshments" after a hard day's work.

In February of 1921, Ogdensburg's small police force found itself on trial. Their crime? Trying to do their job.

After a failed police raid on the New York Avenue speakeasy ended with the chief and two of his officers chased out of the building by drunk pool cue wielding Brenno family members and their supporters to the delighted cheers and jeers of a neighborhood mob, an outraged City Council launched a formal investigation into the events surrounding the breakdown of law and order that had left Ogdensburg's civic image tarnished and the community's law enforcement agency's reputation badly damaged.

The Ogdensburg City Council's Police Committee conducted a formal hearing with prominent attorneys interrogating witnesses to help piece together a picture of what happened that scandalous winter night in the Maple City.

Ogdensburg taxi cab driver George Perry found himself a first hand and major eye witness in the city-wide investigation into the events at the "Red Devil Pool Hall" that led to the city's small police force at the center of the investigation into what was described as the poorly executed police raid on the notorious after-hours pool hall and speakeasy that forced the community to eventually invest in a more professional and better trained police force.

Perry, wearing a bloodied bandage to his head from wounds he suffered from trying to help the police during the incident, testified before the special Ogdensburg city council police committee that he had originally been called to the city police station, located in those days at the town of Oswegatchie and city of Ogdensburg owned municipal Opera House and City Hall at the corner of Ford and Caroline Street earlier in the evening of Wednesday, February 9th, 1921 to pick up Chief McCormick, Sgt. McDonal and Officer Beach as well as Deputy Sheriffs Edward McElligott and Thomas Preston.

According to Perry's testimony, reported in the Feb. 11th edition of the Ogdensburg Republican Journal, the chief told him to drive to the Ford Avenue home of Sim Hayes, another taxi driver, after Mrs. Hayes told police she had been warned that an attempt would be made during the night to rob her house.[20]

Chief McCormick later testified that Mrs. Hayes feared that robbers were looking for a load of liquor they had heard was hidden inside her house. She called the police, asking for protection.

He also testified that while he and his officers were waiting for the taxi to arrive to pick them up, he received a telephone message from Pine Street and Madison Avenue, stating that Mr. Lajoy's residence had been entered and burglarized.

The taxi driver drove the officers a block from the Hayes house when the chief told him to stop.

Officer McDonall and Deputy Preston got out and started toward the Hayes' house and the car went on.

At the corner of Pine Street and Mansion Avenue, the chief told

---

[20] Ogdensburg Republican Journal, Feb. 11, 1921

Perry to stop, and the three officers got out and talked with two men who Perry did not recognize.

Leaving the deputies to guard the Hayes residence, Chief McCormick told Perry to drive to Fraser's near the trolley car barns at the end of New York Avenue, which he did.

The chief and McDonal got out and returned a few minutes later. The party then turned around and started for Cousineau's store which housed the Coleman pool room, also known as the "Red Devil Poolroom" a favorite gathering place for Ogdensburg's Brenno gang. The chief did not say who was suspected of planning the robbery of the Hayes house, but he said that "the Brennos" might be in Cousineau's store and were suspected of being involved in a series of liquor hijackings and robberies across the Second Ward.

When the police arrived, Perry testified, it was obvious a disturbance had been going on inside and that broken glass was scattered over the sidewalk.

The officers got out of the taxicab and went inside.

From his vantage point on New York Avenue, Perry could see four or five men inside the place which served as a neighborhood store, but also offered an afterhours pool room where rumor had it that liquor could be purchased by those in the know.

As the two police officers entered the notorious speakeasy, Perry noticed Sgt. McDonal was already holding his handcuffs in his hands.

While the Cousineau family owned the store, they leased a portion to the Colemans who operated the poolroom. "Leasing" out pool rooms and spare rooms for speakeasies had grown increasingly popular as a way for building owners to avoid the legal risk of having the federal government confiscate their buildings for violating the Prohibition laws.

After the owner of the Oswegatchie Hotel (later known as Chapple's Hotel at the corner of Main and Lake Streets), nearly lost his building in federal court for operating an illegal bar in flagrant violation of the anti-liquor laws, anyone who owned a building would lease the premises to an illegal speakeasy which insulated the property owner from the legal repercussions of allowing illegal booze sales from occurring under his nose.

Frank Coleman, brother of William Coleman, proprietor of the pool room, testified he had been inside the Red Devil Pool Hall Club that night with a group of regulars that included Jimmy and Goldie Brenno, Joe Amo, Lloyd Lundy, King O'Neil, and himself.

Coleman testified the pool hall crowd had been drinking, but he insisted that the Red Devil Pool Hall was not a speakeasy, did not sell liquor or provide it to those who frequented the place.

How they got the liquor was a mystery to him, he told the city council panel, but he freely admitted that the group had been enjoying themselves up until the police arrived.

On this evening, the Red Devil Pool Hall's customers had grown increasingly rowdy as the liquor flowed with the two Brenno brothers, James and Goldie, a part-time professional boxer, wrestling each other. The Brennos had even broken a window, scattering glass outside.

Coleman said the fracas inside the poolroom had grown so intense, he decided the better part of valor was to quietly slip out of the poolroom before he found himself mixed up in even wilder shenanigans.

When Police Chief McCormick, Sgt. McDonal and Officer Beach entered, armed with revolvers and billy clubs, the Red Devil Pool Hall regulars were already in a wild mood.

When the officers entered the poolroom, they grabbed Jimmy Brenno, who demanded to know why they wanted him.

The police told him they had a warrant for his arrest.

Brenno demanded to see the arrest warrant, asking what he was being charged with.

OSWEGATCHIE TOWN AND CITY OF OGDENSBURG MUNICIPAL OFFICES,
OPERA HOUSE AND POLICE STATION
(DESTROYED BY FIRE IN 1926 AND REPLACED BY CURRENT CITY HALL AT THE
CORNER OF FORD AND CAROLINE STREET) (AUTHOR'S COLLECTION)

Chief McCormick told him the police had not brought the arrest warrant with them, but it was back at the Opera House and Jimmy would have a chance to see it when he was brought to the police station.

Fifty years later, in an interview with the Ogdensburg Advance News, Jimmy Brenno offered his own version of the events from a half century before.

In the Sunday, Sept. 7, 1975, edition of the Advance News, Jimmy Brenno told Advance News reporter George Moffat that he believed the police had mistaken him for his brother, William Brenno, who was also no stranger to Ogdensburg's criminal justice system.

William was wanted on a parole violation after having been let out early after serving a sentence in Dannemora State Prison for stealing a wagon load of coal from the Ogdensburg coal yards on the city's St. Lawrence River shoreline.

In the 1920s, coal and wood were the most popular sources of fuel for home heating.

While the watchmen at the coal yards were known to occasionally look the other way when poor families filled their pockets with coal to heat their homes, the company drew the line at people stealing wagon loads of coal and selling it to their friends and neighbors at a lower price than the company offered.

William Brenno's arrest and prosecution had served as an object lesson to Ogdensburg's criminal underworld on what could happen if someone tried to compete with the coal company by using its own product to sell at a discounted rate.

So, James Brenno had serious doubts that the police really had a warrant with his name on it back at the police station.

Plus, he and his friends just were not quite ready to end their evening out in the town just because of a case of mistaken identity.

That is why he told the Advance News 50 years later he pushed back when Sgt. McDonal grabbed him by the shirt.

Brenno recounted that when the officer grabbed him and tore his shirt, he lost his temper and punched the police officer in the side of the face.

When Officer Beach pulled out his nightstick to club him into submission, Brenno grabbed it and wrestled it out of the officer's hands.

Perry testified he heard someone inside shout, "Don't hit him or we'll kill you" when Beach raised his club.

Witnesses described Brenno as a stockily built, muscular young man, with a dark complexion and heavy black hair he brushed back over his head.

Brenno used the billy club to strike McDonal a glancing blow on the arm, causing the officer to release his hold, The officers later admitted that Brenno was just too powerful for them to subdue and after he had grabbed the riot baton, they were unable to take him into custody.

OGDENSBURG'S PINE STREET NEIGHBORHOOD (AUTHOR'S COLLECTION)

Sgt. McDonal testified under questioning that he was 61 years old. He claimed that there were 8 to 10 people inside the pool room when the police conducted the raid. McDonal testified after the melee was over Officer Beach complained that his heart was bothering him.

When he was asked why he did not use his billy club to subdue Brenno after Jimmy took Officer Beach's night stick from him, Sgt. McDonal replied slowly, "If we had done so, we would now be in the morgue."

With his officers in trouble, Chief McCormick drew his revolver, but the members of the Brenno gang, seeing their leader was being ganged up on, were menacing the officers with pool cues to defend the honor of the Red Devil Pool Hall.

Officer Beach testified after Sgt. McDonal. He testified he counted twelve men in the place at the time of the raid. One of them swung at him with a cue stick and he heard Jimmy Brenno shout to his men, "Knock their blocks off."

Beach testified he and McDonal were unable to subdue Jimmy Brenno.

"They (the members of the Brenno gang) were all interfering with us," he testified. "They kicked us and thumped us."

Officer Beach said he saw one man with a gun but he himself thought it best not to pull his gun and shoot during the confrontation, for fear of starting a gunfight if members of the Brenno gang were carrying concealed weapons.

He testified the police would have needed six or eight men to handle the Brenno gang.

Brenno would later claim that he swiped the gun from Chief McCormick's hand in an article in the Advance News in the 1970s, but testimony in front of the police committee in 1921 did not support his claim.

Taxi driver Perry testified that a crowd had quickly gathered outside the pool hall, drawn by the noise and excitement as news spread in the upper New York Avenue neighborhood that the city police had raided the Brenno gang's "Red Devil Pool Club" and notorious neighborhood speakeasy.

The cab driver claimed the crowd was clearly in support of the Brennos, especially Jimmy Brenno, with one person in the crowd clearly agitated over the possible arrest of the well-known neighborhood tough guy.

The man, who Perry claimed was named either "Fuzzy" or "Pussy," was upset over the idea of Jimmy Brenno being taken into custody.

The cab driver testified he saw the man was carrying a pistol and heard him tell someone else in the crowd, "If they take Brenno out of here, they will go out dead."

City Councilor Albert D. Cordwell presided over the special hearing with members of the Police Committee, including Alderman H. B. Wallace and C. S. Hubbard conducting the investigation into the events that had embarrassed the police force.

Attorney D. W. Mulligan had been designated by Mayor Lynch as special city attorney. He conducted the examination of witnesses. Corporation Counsel R. K. Waterman sat in for part of the session.

Mayor Edward P. Lynch also sat in for a part of the hearing, asking questions to some of the witnesses.

While the members of the Police Committee did not tell reporters what their recommendations might be, the Ogdensburg Republican Journal reported "there was a feeling that the disclosures made during the hearing, coupled with the criticism of the police department" made by members of the Common Council on Wednesday night gave the distinct impression that the hearing "would undoubtedly lead to the biggest shakeup that the force has known in years."[21]

---

[21] Ogdensburg Republican Journal, Feb. 11, 1921

NOTORIOUS SPEAKEASY - IN 1921, THIS BUILDING AT THE CORNER OF NEW YORK AVE-
NUE AND PINE STREET HOUSED WHAT WAS ONCE THE NOTORIOUS WESTSIDE
SPEAKEASY KNOWN AS THE "RED DEVIL POOL HALL." THE RIGHT-HAND SIDE HOUSED
COUSINEAU'S NEIGHBORHOOD STORE WHICH HAD FORMERLY HOUSED THE A&P.
OGDENSBURG'S PINE STREET NEIGHBORHOOD (AUTHOR'S COLLECTION)

Councilors told reporters the hearing had been held to investigate whether officers "had exercised due diligence and the necessary force to uphold the law."

The taxi driver told the city council that Chief McCormick stepped out of the poolroom with his gun drawn, menacing the onlookers, and ordering the crowd back. The chief ordered the cab driver to come into the poolroom to help his officers subdue Brenno, but before Perry could go to the assistance of the officers, someone in the crowd struck him from behind in the back of the head with what he believed was a lead pipe, dropping him to his knees.

"The weapon looked" like "a piece of lead pipe, three and a half or four inches long," he said.

Perry said his assailant raised his arm to strike him again, but the taxicab driver tackled the thug by the legs and threw him off his balance. His attacker dropped his weapon and ran. "I called to the chief," he testified." I said, 'there goes the man that hit me! Shoot him! '"

But Perry said that even though the chief had his pistol in his hand, instead of shooting his attacker, "the chief replied, 'Perry, you are awful excited.'""

Perry said he did not know the name of the man who hit him but said he would recognize him if he saw him again. The chief ran around the corner of the building after his attacker, but the man had fled the scene.

Jimmy Brenno also used the confusion to escape into the crowd, carrying the police billy club that belonged to Officer Beach.

Bleeding from his head wound, and still stunned from the blow to his head, Perry testified he spotted Benny Daniels, another taxi man, who had driven up in his vehicle to watch the excitement.

Perry, bleeding from his wound to the head, called to his fellow cabdriver and asked for his help, urging him to summon assistance, telling him "They were murdering people."

Daniels sped off downtown to gather whatever help he could find.

With Brenno gone, Chief McCormick gathered his men together and told Perry to drive them back to the police station.

As they were crossing the Lafayette-Spring Street Bridge, the police met taxicab driver Daniels who was returning with St. Lawrence County District Attorney William D. Ingram, who lived in Ogdensburg.

Ingram, a no-nonsense career prosecutor, who had worked his way up into his post after serving an apprenticeship as chief assistant under former District Attorney James C. Dolan, was not amused at the idea that police officers had been mocked and forced to back down from their job. After a conference with the chief in which the

DA heard what had transpired, Ingram told Perry to seek medical attention and ordered everyone else into his cab to return to the upper New York Avenue neighborhood to attempt to find Brenno and Perry's assailant.

In his newspaper interview 50 years later, Brenno told the Advance News he had returned to his home on Pine Street with the police billy club he had stolen from Officer Beach. He told his mother what had happened, but when the police came looking for him, he was hiding under her porch.

After Perry had his head wound dressed by a doctor, he also went back to the scene of the trouble to see if he could identify his assailant. It was midnight but there was still a crowd in front of the speakeasy. Perry did not see the man who hit him, but he spied a youth in khaki, who, he thought, was standing near him when he was struck from behind. Perry asked him if he knew who his assailant was, but the youth replied that he did not, claiming he had been at home all night and only recently arrived to see what the commotion was all about. The district attorney took the youth in khaki aside and walked him up the street to question him privately.

Perry said he then drove the party to the Hayes place where they picked up the Sheriff's deputies McElligott and Preston, Perry was then taken home.

After failing to find anyone, Ingram directed police to arrest Frank Coleman in connection with running a disorderly establishment.

The DA also hired Ogdensburg private detective Frank Gladle to search for Brenno.

Gladle confronted Brenno at the poolroom later in the evening after the excitement in the neighborhood had died down and Brenno had returned to the location.

But the private eye had no better luck taking Brenno into custody.

Brenno, an experienced Second Ward Street fighter, quickly made short work of the detective.

The following day, officers returned to the upper New York Avenue and Pine Street neighborhood, searching for the elusive Brennos.

When they saw two of the Brennos leaving a house and fleeing after spotting the police, the police fired several shots at them, but the brothers escaped.

Chief McCormick was called to the stand and testified he believed there were nine or 10 men inside the pool room at the time of the raid.

Under questioning, Chief McCormick admitted that neither officer had a copy of a warrant at the time.

Councilors asked why the officers had failed to use their revolvers to shoot their assailants if they felt threatened during the confrontation.

"The chief testified he was aware that an officer was armed with a revolver to protect himself in the performance of his duty," the newspaper reported.

He also admitted to the police committee that nothing had been done to arrest any of the members of the Brenno gang who interfered in the police raid at the "Red Devil Pool Room."

Chief McCormick testified he drew his revolver to keep the men back when they advanced on his officers with pool cues, but he said he did not believe it was necessary to shoot them. He admitted under questioning that he told the group inside the building he did not want to shoot anyone. He said he did not personally witness Brenno wrestle the billy club out of Officer Beach's hands.

He told the city council committee he thought the officers did the best they could under the circumstances, but insisted they were badly outnumbered.

Under questioning, he testified he had no complaint to make

against Officer Beach, but conceded that a younger, more vigorous officer might have handled the situation better, suggesting that if Officer Nicholson had been with them, the raid might have turned out differently. In answer to a question by Mayor Lynch, the chief said he did not know he had the right to shoot a man to uphold the law.

The chief testified under oath that "Jimmy" Brenno was "too much" for the two of them to handle and that several more officers would have been needed to cope with the fight inside the pool room. The chief insisted his officers were doing everything possible to put an end to the thievery and wave of lawlessness plaguing neighborhoods in the city, but admitted his officers had not made much headway. He said the biggest ringleaders suspected of committing these break-ins were "elusive" and "even the New York State Police had failed in their efforts to catch them." The chief admitted that a plain clothes detective to handle investigations would be an immense help.

Attorney Mulligan asked the chief several questions to test his knowledge of the duties of his office and his replies tended to show that he did not truly realize the powers and responsibilities his position entailed. Under questioning from the attorneys and the mayor, Chief McCormick admitted having a limited knowledge of what the law allowed him to do under the circumstances.

He told the police committee he had done the best he could with the officers he had available to him.

"I have done the best I could," the chief said at the end of his public interrogation, "and if I have made mistakes, I am sorry."

When Frank Coleman was called to the stand, he testified he saw no gun carried by anyone in the pool room. He disagreed with Police Committee Chair Cordwell's characterization that the Brennos had gone into hiding. He testified he saw them at a dance in the Fourth Ward.

Mayor Lynch brought the public hearing to a close by requesting the Police committee to bring in a report at a special meeting of the council to be held the next week and added that if conditions warranted it, he would then appoint a special officer to act as a plain clothes detective. On a motion by Alderman Cordwell, the Municipal Civil Service Commission was requested to call another examination for candidates for appointment to the police force.

The police investigation hearing led to the editors of Ogdensburg's Republican Journal to call for the city council to reform the police department by firing the police officers who are" physically unable to carry out their duties in enforcing the law." The editorial in the Feb. 11, 1921, Friday edition of the Republican Journal offered the newspaper's view of what the community and city council needed to do considering what the hearing showed:

WEST SIDE FRACAS.

Investigations are conducted for the purpose of revealing certain facts in connection with certain happenings, and yesterday's investigation on the part of the Police Committee into the West Side fracas of Wednesday night revealed conclusively that the present police department is unable to cope with any out-of-the-ordinary happening.

While the officers who took part in the attempted round-up evidently proceeded along lines which, in their judgment, seemed right, nevertheless the fact remains that they lost their prisoner, lost a nightstick, and finally, lost their reputation as preservers of the law.

That the present police department is entirely inadequate as regards physical strength, was admitted by the officers under oath, and any further investigation will simply tend to make the department a greater fiasco.

The city fathers must be aware— and are aware—that there is great chance for improvement in this important department of our civic government, and it is apparent that there remains but one thing to do—retire those officers who are unable to cope with a situation the like of which arose Wednesday night.

Replace the older men with young and fearless blood— men who can and will preserve order, and who will give the taxpayers a run for their money in the preservation of law and order.

While Chief McCormick undoubtedly is doing the best he knows how, the investigation revealed that he falls far short in those characteristics which should be found in a man occupying such a responsible position.

The city fathers are the representatives of the people, elected and placed in office for the fulfillment of duties pertaining to our civic government. Wednesday night's fracas and yesterday's Police Committee investigation revealed the fact that there is one most important and urgent duty— and that is to cause an immediate reorganization of the Police Department. And the quicker steps are taken in this direction the more satisfied the taxpayers will be.

In the Monday Feb. 14th edition of the Syracuse Post Standard, Ogdensburg found its troubles with the Brenno gang had gained statewide attention with an article in the major Central New York publication proclaiming the Maple City was facing a reign of terror with daily riots and outbreaks of violence that authorities were unable to handle on their own.

The Post Standard reported:

OGDENSBURG, Feb. 13—Two state troopers have been sent to Ogdensburg to take charge of the terrorist situation until the city can readjust itself and get its own police force back on a normal basis.

St. Lawrence County District Attorney William Ingram has decided to take official action against Chief of Police McCormick unless the latter resigns at once. The chief, it is understood, is willing to quit and is preparing his resignation to be handed to Mayor Lynch at Wednesday night's council meeting. These two developments were the only ones which affected the police situation. Saturday night was quiet and there were no outbreaks to disturb the usual Sunday calm of the city.

While the citizens of Ogdensburg have not returned to their usual ways of doing things, there is still a disposition to watch for sudden gang outbreaks in the western part of the city. Ogdensburg, in the main, has practically resumed its usual round of affairs. Rumors that some of the citizens had been forming a secret "vigilantes" committee to patrol the streets themselves was heard here this afternoon. As far as could be learned, however, no such organization has been formed and none is yet projected. However, several citizens have volunteered to act as special police in any raid on the Pine street gang that may be planned.

Investigation from the district attorney's office and of an unofficial nature has failed to bring to light anything which may connect the incendiary fire of Saturday with the Brenno gang, said to be the crowd which first brought the disturbances in the city to a head. The fires were set, without a doubt, however. The state troopers have been requested through District Attorney Ingram's office and with the approval, it is understood, of the mayor. They are scheduled to arrive late tonight and will be placed in control of the situation. It is believed they will head a concerted drive against the Pine street gang, either tomorrow afternoon or evening.

The officials believe the state police will be able to stem the tide of terror. The city will give the state police carte blanche and will order to their assistance any men they may need. Ingram, according to information from his office, asked for them with the avowed purpose of having them arrest the leaders of the terror gangs. He hopes through them to eliminate the leaders and thus stop the rioting and disorder which have been going on in a general way for four days.

The railroad detectives, whose presence in the city was made known Friday night, and who searched the Pine Street section for evidence of thefts from railroad property, left this city hurriedly late last night.

They did not say where they went or why, but it is believed here they may bring to light something that will connect a few of the alleged gang members with wider plots against law and order.

In the Tuesday, Feb. 15th edition of the Republican Journal, Ogdensburg's own daily went out of its way to condemn the Syracuse newspaper's version of events. The Republican Journal condemned the Monday article in the Syracuse Post Standard in the strongest terms:

SYRACUSE TALE REPUDIATED
Mayor Protests Against "Gross Exaggerations" In Outside Paper
DISTRICT ATTORNEY ADDS DENIAL

A sensational story dealing with crime conditions alleged to exist in Ogdensburg, which appeared in the Syracuse Post-Standard yesterday under an Ogdensburg date line, brought denials from Mayor Edward P. Lynch and District Attorney William D. Ingram.

The mayor was quoted as saying that he "would clean up the city police force" if the city council backed him up at the council meeting tomorrow night.

The Syracuse daily claimed state troopers "have been detailed to Ogdensburg" and that "District Attorney Ingram has definitely decided to take official action against Chief of Police McCormick unless the latter resigns at once."

Both the mayor" and the District Attorney denied that the state police had been ordered here or that their presence had been requested and the District Attorney also denied that he had decided to move against Chief McCormick unless he quit his office. The District Attorney added, however, that he might lay the matter before the grand jury if the Common Council took no action.

Mayor Lynch pointed out that the State police could not be ordered here without his 'assent' and that such action had never been considered.

The mayor dismissed what he described as "the wild and reckless statements which have been appearing in the Syracuse paper" since the pool room fracas on the west side last Wednesday night. He said that these statements were gross exaggerations and that they tended to give the city a bad reputation without cause.

Mayor Lynch denied he had discussed with anyone police or crime conditions growing out of the affair last Wednesday night and that any expression of opinion purporting to come from him on the subject was unauthorized and without foundation.

The interview that appeared in the Syracuse paper reported:

The Post Standard had reported in its Feb. 14th edition:

"If the city council will back me up, I will clean up the city police force at Wednesday night's meeting."

This was the promise of Edward P. Lynch tonight after a personal trip through the Pine Street section.

"I found conditions deplorable," he said. "They are as bad, if not worse, than they have been reported. I am determined to clean up the city."

In his interview with the Republican Journal, Mayor Lynch denied he had made "a personal trip through the Pine Street section."

In the same Feb, 15 edition, the Republican Journal reported two of the Ogdensburg gangsters had been captured by the long arm of the law.

LUMBER CAMP NEAR DeGRASSE IN EARLY 1900s

BRENNO BROTHERS CAUGHT BY SHERIFF AND TROOPERS, PAIR QUICKLY SURRENDERS

Arrests Made at Hermon Following Arrival of Brothers After Few Days Stay at Lumber Camps; Were Enroute to Ogdensburg to Give Themselves Up, They Said, James Will Be Brought to Ogdensburg and His Brother Will Be Taken to Dannemora Prison

James and William Brenno, alleged to be ringleaders of a gang which is charged with committing a series of depredations on Ogdensburg's West side during the past few months and who succeeded in evading arrest when a raid was made on a Second Ward speak easy and pool room by the police last Wednesday night, were arrested yesterday afternoon at Hermon as they were on their way from a lumber camp near DeGrasse in the foothills of the Adirondacks.[22]

HERMON DOWNTOWN POST OFFICE IN 1920S (PUBLIC DOMAIN)

---

[22] Ogdensburg Republican Journal, Feb. 15, 1921

Word to this effect was received late yesterday afternoon by District Attorney William D. Ingram from Sheriff Lawrence Fishbeck, who, with a party of state troopers, made the arrests.

The Brennos were taken to Canton and lodged in the county jail, Sheriff Fishbeck said.

The Sheriff and Sergeant Rauth of the state constabulary and another trooper arrested the men at 3 p.m. in front of the post office at Hermon as they got off the Russell stage.

The troopers were in uniform. Sheriff Fishbeck walked up to the Brenno brothers and said, "Boys, you are under arrest."

"All right, Sheriff," they said, "we will go with you."

The men were placed in the car and brought to the Canton jail without any difficulty. Sheriff Fishbeck said the men were not handcuffed. At the jail, the men were searched but no weapons were found on them.

DANNEMORA PRISON (1920s) (WIKIMEDIA)

They told the sheriff they had been at Clifton for two or three days and walked to Russell, where they intended to stage the stage from Hermon.

They said that they were on their way to Ogdensburg to give themselves up to the local police.

Upon receiving word that the Brenno brothers had gone to the lumber camps, District Attorney Ingram called up the sheriff and the state troopers at Canton yesterday morning and directed them to try to capture the pair.

The arrests were made without difficulty, the brothers accompanying the officers peaceably.

As soon as County Probation Officer John M. Nichols heard of the arrests, he called up the warden of the state prison at Dannemora, where William Brenno was wanted for breaking his parole, and requested that an officer be sent for him.

The warden replied that a keeper would arrive at Canton tonight to take Brenno back to prison.

James Brenno will be brought to Ogdensburg today for arraignment before City Judge Corcoran on a charge of grand larceny.

Probation Officer Nichols states that William Brenno will have to serve about a year at Dannemora before he is released. He was originally sentenced to serve an indeterminate term for burglary but was placed on probation. He was later returned by the probation officer for sentence for breaking probation and was committed to Dannemora. After serving part of his term, he was released on parole, which he subsequently violated, and a warrant has been out for him on that charge since a year ago last January.

In the same newspaper, William Coleman wrote that he objected to the "Red Devil" nickname for his poolroom that had been reported in the Ogdensburg News, a competing city newspaper.

The headline reported:

Objects to Slang Names

"I wish you would tell the public that my pool room and confectionery store was never called the "Red Devil" or the "Devil's Oven," as it is known as the Red Front on account of the A. & P. Store being in business there before I started. All this slang was in The Ogdensburg News. There were no windows, doors or chairs broken while the officers were in my place. (Signed)

WILLIAM COLEMAN

The Feb. 16th edition of the Republican Journal recounted James Brenno's return to the city for a court hearing after his apprehension in Hermon and detention in the St. Lawrence County Jail.

James Brenno was brought back to Ogdensburg by Deputy Sheriff Edward McElligott and Police Sgt Charles Harper. The courtroom was jammed with spectators when Brenno was brought up for arraignment. After Brenno had been assigned to a chair in the courtroom, City Judge Corcoran told him: "Welcome to our city, James," and then proceeded to read the complaint which was sworn to by Officer McDonal, whom Brenno was charged with resisting when the police sought to arrest him during the raid on the Coleman pool room a week ago.[23]

Brenno called for counsel and asked that Attorney R. C. Sanford represent him.

Mr. Sanford held a short conference with the defendant and then waived examination. District Attorney Ingram represented the people.

Brenno's mother and other relatives were present in the courtroom.

---

[23] Ogdensburg Republican Journal, Feb. 16, 1921

A reporter wrote that "there was nothing desperate looking about him. He wore a soft shirt, blue coat, black corduroy trousers with patches on the knees and tan shoes."

The bail was fixed at $500. (Equivalent to $8,000 in today's 2024 dollars,) Working men earned about $3,200 a year in 1922. A modest house cost $6,200.

On Feb. 25th, the Ogdensburg City Council presented its anxiously awaited report on how the community should deal with its aging police force in the face of an increasingly violent criminal element that had little respect for the law.

The report served as a call for action and reform as Ogdensburg prepared itself to deal with the problems that Prohibition was causing in the community.

The Feb. 26th, 1921, Republican Journal's publication of the Police Committee report stunned the community:

POLICE REPORT SUMMARY.

- Officers are physically unfit to act as patrolmen.
- The Chief used poor judgment in handling the disturbance.
- Prompt and effective action is needed to suppress lawlessness.
- Police force should be reorganized
- Salaries should be increased.
- The department should be increased to eight patrolmen.
- The records system should be more comprehensive.

The report of the Police Committee on its investigation into the circumstances surrounding the disturbance at Coleman's pool room on New York Avenue on the night of Feb. 9th was submitted at the meeting of the Common Council which was held last night.

The committee found that Chief McCormick used "poor judgment" and Officers McDonal and Beach, veteran members of the force, who accompanied him, are physically unfit to act as patrolmen.

That the force should "be reorganized, salaries increased, the patrol force increased to eight men and a better system of keeping police records must be adopted.

The report was passed without dissent following a discussion in which Mayor Lynch and several of the aldermen took part. The Police Committee will now draft a plan of reorganization for submission to the Council. On motion of Alderman Hubbard, the mayor was authorized to appoint two special patrolmen to serve until such time as permanent selections are made from the eligible list.

THE COMMITTEE'S REPORT:

The report of the Police Committee was as follows:

Ogdensburg, N. Y., Feb. 14, 1921.
To the Honorable Mayor and Common Council: Your committee appointed to investigate the Police Department present the following report, findings, and recommendations:

On the 10th of February 1921, at 2 o'clock in the afternoon, the committee with Attorney Daniel W. Mulligan, acting counsel, and John M. Morley, court stenographer, met in the council rooms for the purpose of determining and procuring evidence on the raid on New York Avenue on the evening of February 9th.

The following persons were examined:

- George Perry, taxi driver
- Officer John McDonal
- Officer Frank Beach
- Chief of Police John McCormick
- Frank Coleman

The committee does not feel it is necessary to give a full report of the evidence taken as it has been published in the daily press.

It appears that on the evening of February 9th, between the hours of 9 and 10 o'clock, Chief McCormick received a communication from Sim Hayes who resides on Ford Avenue, stating that his wife had received information that their residence was to be burglarized that evening, and desired police protection.

The chief immediately proceeded to get what available force he had together, consisting of Officers McDonal, Beach, Constable McElligott, and Thomas Preston, and called for a taxi at the cab stand to call for them at police headquarters.

While waiting for the taxi he received a telephone message from Pine Street and Madison Avenue, stating that Mr. Lajoy's residence had been entered and burglarized. As soon as the taxi arrived, they proceeded to Ford Avenue near the residence of Mr. Hayes.

Later, when officers entered a poolroom at the corner of New York Avenue and Pine Street, Officer Beach entered the building with Officer McDonal, when several of the persons in the building attacked and interfered with the officers, whereupon Chief McCormick went to the assistance of the officers by keeping the crowd from interfering.

It appears that in the struggle between Officers McDonal and

Beach, and James Brenno, Officer Beach had his club forcibly taken away from him, and James Brenno made his escape.

George Perry, the taxi driver, while standing next to his car, was assaulted by some unknown person with a club or piece of iron pipe, and cut on the head, the culprit getting away, there being no further disturbance.

The officers entered the taxi and proceeded down New York avenue. At the junction of New York Avenue and Spring Street they met an automobile with District Attorney William D. Ingram. They halted, and at the request of the district attorney, they entered his car and proceeded with him to Pine Street and Ford Avenue to the residence of Frank Coleman, who on the orders of the district attorney, was placed under arrest, then they all returned to police headquarters.

Findings

"Upon the evidence procured, your committee finds:

- 1st. That upon the testimony adduced, the officers are physically unfit to discharge the duties of patrolmen.
- 2nd. That the chief used poor judgment in handling the disturbance. As an officer of the law, he had a right to impress any or all persons for assistance.
- 3rd. That the conditions existing in the upper Second Ward demand prompt and effective action by the mayor and proper authorities, regardless of expense, to put down this lawlessness.

Your committee makes the following recommendations: [24]

---

[24] Ogdensburg Republican Journal, Feb. 26, 1921

- 1st. That the police force of the city of Ogdensburg be reorganized.
- 2nd. That the salaries of the chief of police and the policemen be such that men of good moral character, and mental and physical abilities may be induced to apply for positions.
- 3rd. That the number of police officers eligible for patrol duty should be eight men.
- 4th. That a more comprehensive system of records should be adopted in the police department.

Committee: A. CORDWELL, C. S. HUBBARD, HOWARD B. WALLACE.

The report, which was agreed to by the entire Police Committee, was presented by Chairman Albert Cordwell, who parenthetically remarked after reading the findings that it was "regrettable that the newspaper hero" of the occasion had not been present during the trouble as all it would have been necessary for him to have done was to have ordered Brenno, the man who escaped, to hold out his hands and then snap the bracelets onto his wrists. Alderman Webb moved that the report be accepted and that its recommendations be carried out, which was carried without objection following a brief discussion.

Mayor Lynch stated that a hefty sum was raised by tax to maintain the police force and that it was a department of city government that was nearer than any other to the people.

Years ago, he continued, the city possessed a good force, made up of men who did their duty and were proud of their positions. The position of police officer, he stated, was a dignified and important one and the relation which the police officer bore to the people, so far as he was individually concerned, was just as important as that of an alderman or any other member of the city government. What the department needed above all, he went on, was harmony of action and spirit. The officers who have grievances should go to the proper authorities with them and not take it upon themselves to go behind their backs and criticize.

In conclusion, the mayor said: "To the members of the Police Committee I desire to say that I will back them to the limit in getting a force that will appeal to the taxpayers and the law-abiding people of the city."

Alderman Pearson said that there were some things in the report that he approved and others that he did not. He declared that it was impossible to maintain an efficient force at the salaries paid. Some of the officers are now past the age for active service but they have done good and effective work in the past, and he believed that provision should be made for them.

Mayor Lynch remarked that the conditions in the police department were not of recent development but had existed during the past four or five years. Continuing his remarks, Alderman Pearson said the trouble that occurred on the night of Feb. 9th was an accident and that the police should not be censured as they had done the best they could under the circumstances. "No good citizen has protested to me regarding what occurred or recommended that these officers be removed," said the alderman. He suggested the committee might have been a little more specific in its recommendations. Chairman Cordwell, in defending the report, said the police had been criticized and justly so. Conditions in the department, he asserted, had been a reproach to the city for the last ten or fifteen years. "It is up to us how to improve them or quit," he declared. "Citizens are demanding improvements. Are we to 'Let George do it,' as the saying is. To paraphrase the poet, "are councils to come and go while the police department goes on forever?"

A ripple of applause greeted the alderman's remarks. Alderman Wallace stated that he had no grievance against the chief or the other officers, but the question to consider was whether these men were not too old for further active service. He knew they had done excellent work in the past and was not in favor of retiring them without some compensation.

Mayor Lynch stated that under the charter, the city was not empowered to provide a pension fund for its employees. He said in the past sentiment and other considerations had operated to keep officers in service long after they had reached the retiring age and became disqualified for active service. "Efficiency' must not give way to sentiment, however, if we are to effect improvements," said the mayor.

Alderman Wallace said the police should be always prepared to perform police duty and he believed they were on the night in question as they were armed with clubs and guns.

Alderman Wallace asked for information regarding the decision to hire outside counsel to assist the Police Committee in their investigation into the west side fracas.

The mayor said that in the case of the police investigation, he had taken the matter up with the members of the Police Committee and that they had agreed to hire outside counsel.

The Feb. 18th, edition of the Republican Journal the editors offered their thoughts on the numerous letters from detective agencies, individuals and groups who were offering to come to Ogdensburg to "clean up" the city if the local police force was unable. ***

"The publicity given throughout the state to the recent police fracas in this city has resulted in Mayor Lynch receiving scores of letters from applicants for the job of 'cleaning up' the town, the various writers claiming that they possess special qualifications for jobs of this kind. Some of the letters come from professional detective agencies, which state that they can bring a large force of strong-arm men here to give the town a going over that would make it vie with the famed spotless 'burg of song and story. While none of the writers intended to be humorous, their suggestions and offer of assistance in making Ogdensburg "a safe place to live in" are nevertheless good antidotes for dull care and make excellent light reading for His Honor when the worries of office begin to weigh heavily. So much for those "write ups of statewide importance."

District Attorney Ingram indicted Brenno in the May term.

Four months after the February speakeasy raid, James Brenno appeared before St. Lawrence County Court Judge John C. Crapser, a former District Attorney.

St. Lawrence County's District Attorney Ingram quickly secured an indictment against Jimmy Brenno.

But Brenno had secured the services of Herman J. Donovan, a prominent Ogdensburg attorney, who argued that the police had no business attempting to arrest his client since they failed to produce the warrant, they claimed was back at the police station.

St. Lawrence County Judge John Crapser surprised many people across the North Country when he issued his ruling in the controversial Jimmy Brenno case

In the June 9th edition of the Ogdensburg Republican Journal, St. Lawrence County Court Judge John Crapser ruled in favor of Jimmy Brenno, dismissing the indictment and ruling that the Ogdensburg man could not be charged with resisting arrest when officers had testified that they failed to show him the warrant for his arrest when he asked to see it.[25]

In a major victory, Attorney Donovan successfully asked the court to dismiss the indictment and throw the charges against Brenno out on the grounds that the officer making the arrest, when asked by Brenno to show his warrant, stated that he did not have it with him.

In granting the motion, Judge Crapser laid down the following rules law enforcement needed to follow when making arrests.

"The court rules that a peace officer may arrest a person without a warrant, when a felony has been committed, in fact, and he has reasonable cause to believe the person he is arresting committed it," Judge Crapser wrote. "But when an officer states to a defendant that he is being placed under arrest by reason of a warrant, such officer must, if demanded by the person to be arrested, produce the warrant, or have it with him; that an officer having knowledge that a felony has been committed by the fact that a warrant has been issued, although the possession of the warrant was in some other person, can arrest the defendant by stating to him that he is an officer and that he arrests such defendant for a felony, but that if an officer approaches a man and says he arrests him by virtue of a warrant, that such officer must then have the warrant with him and must show such warrant to such defendant if the defendant then demands it."

"The uncontradicted facts in this case show that the officer did not say to the defendant Brenno that he was arresting him for a felony but that the facts in the' case show that the officer said to the defen-

---

[25] Ogdensburg Republican Journal, June 9, 1921

dant Brenno that he arrested him on a warrant and that therefore the defendant had a right to see said warrant, having been informed that he was arrested on a warrant, before he can be charged with resisting an officer. By section 173 of the code of criminal procedure, it is provided that a defendant is to be informed by the officer that he acts under the authority of a warrant and such officer must produce and show the warrant to the defendant if the defendant so requires as the defendant did in this case."

The District Attorney disagreed with the court's interpretation of the law, taking the broad ground that an officer, having "reasonable ground" to believe that a felony has been committed and that the person to be arrested was the guilty party, had the right to make the arrest without having the warrant in his personal possession at the time of the arrest. The prosecutor stated he would study the opinion carefully before deciding if he would take steps to appeal Judge Crapser's ruling to have it examined by higher courts. District Attorney Ingram quickly had police arrest Brenno on new charges in connection with the separate fight that also occurred at Cousineau's store on New York Avenue later that night when Ogdensburg private detective Frank Gladle attempted to take James into custody the same night, he had been hired by the District Attorney to search the neighborhood for him.

Brenno was brought back to Ogdensburg to face a misdemeanor third degree assault charge in city court for beating up the private detective that had been sent to capture him. But the misdemeanor charge was also thrown out when Attorney Donovan argued the private detective had no authority to try to take Brenno into custody because police had no legal right to be pursuing him in the first place, much less sending a private detective after him.

The Republican Journal wrote "the Brenno affair caused an upheaval in police circles and formed the basis for highly colored articles that were printed in an out-of-town newspaper about a "crime wave" in Ogdensburg that the local daily newspaper argued were manufactured in a competing publication.

"These tales were written in the office of the paper that published them. The most sensational of the lot was one stating that the Mayor and District Attorney had asked for the assistance of the state police to suppress "outlawry," the Journal wrote. "The police department was investigated because of the hue and cry and a report recently brought in recommended that Officers McDonal and Beach, who failed to apprehend Brenno, be dismissed. Chief McCormick, who accompanied the two officers, was also declared in the report "to be unacquainted with the duties of his office. At the time of the arrest and ever since, some lawyers who have examined the affair have expressed the opinion that the police erred in going after Brenno without a warrant," the Journal argued. "As a matter of fact, there has always been a question as to whether a warrant ever had been issued for his arrest."

AN OGDENSBURG ATTORNEY'S FEE IN 1921

Fifty years later, Jimmy Brenno recounted his version of what happened the night he became a Second Ward and Maple City legend. In the Sunday, September 7, 1975, edition of the Ogdensburg Advance News, the newspaper reported that Brenno, who the newspaper now described as "a respectable householder of Morristown" that attorney Herman Donovan, one of the most respected counselors of the city, visited Jim in his county jail cell and offered to represent him without fee.[26]

Flabbergasted, Jimmy asked, "What do you want to do? Send me to jail?"

"Nope", was the response. "I'll personally guarantee you'll never do a single day."

Counselor Donovan did his work so well that when Jim went to trial on the first assault charge, the judge took the case away from the jury and dismissed the charges without a stain on his character.

When he asked Donovan what he would take as a fee, the attorney replied, "Just a little help in drinking up some Gordon Dry Gin!"

The Advance News columnist wrote of the events 50 years before:

"They do not make lawyers like that anymore! At least, this writer has never met any of them, if they do exist, which he continues to doubt! None of the other charges were ever followed up. However, Mr. Brenno goes on, Ogdensburg's finest were not entirely without their uses at other times. When an overworked bootlegger could not find other transportation for a load of drinkables, he could always whistle up the Black Maria (police van, also known as a paddy wagon) and merely gave the cop in charge a case of beer for the accommodation. Ah! The 'Good Old Days!' Then the North Country was truly prosperous! Oh yes! The cop got his nightstick back, and it had been adorned with a pretty blue ribbon!

---

[26] Advance News, Ogdensburg, Sept. 7, 1975 (Interview with Jimmy Brenno 50 years after incident)

The editors of the Republican Journal and District Attorney Ingram, however, saw matters differently. In the Oct. 17, 1921, edition the newspaper reported that the DA demanded the police chief resign or face indictment. But in their fierce editorial attack on the police department, chief, mayor and city council, the Republican newspaper revealed what was really going on behind the scenes in the battle over the police force. The mayor was refusing to allow the Republicans on city council to name half of any the new police officers appointed to the force. In the era before Civil Service laws protected police from the whims of political machines for their appointment, the newspaper revealed the Republicans were frustrated by Democratic Mayor Lynch's refusal to give them their share of the political appointments to the police force.

DA DEMANDS POLICE CHIEF RESIGN OR FACE INDICTMENT
POLICE MATTERS IN LIMELIGHT AGAIN

Because of his alleged incompetency and dereliction of duty, District Attorney William D. Ingram has issued an ultimatum that Chief of Police J. D. McCormick either resigns or an indictment against him charging neglect of duty will be asked of the next grand jury.

This action on the part of the courageous and fearless prosecuting officer is the result of conditions that have existed in the police department for the past several months, finally culminating in friction between the police department and the district attorney's office.

Several weeks ago, the police committee made an investigation into the police department and finally reported that the chief of police was not sufficiently acquainted with the duties of his office and left the disposition to the discretion of the mayor and Common Council. The report was tabled to the 'disgust of the city people, and nothing further has been done about it. In view of the derelict way Mayor Lynch and the Common Council have acted on its own report, it has finally become necessary for the district attorney's office to take a hand in the matter in the interest of law and order and the protection of the people of the city.

There has never been any question raised as to Mr. McCormick not being an excellent citizen and fine man but as a police officer he is entirely out of his field of usefulness.

There are numerous cases cited by District Attorney Ingram where Chief McCormick has taken upon himself the duties of the district attorney. People who were arrested and placed in jail were later allowed to go after a talk with the chief. None of these people, it is alleged, were even brought before the recorder. Whether there is politics or not in the anticipated shake up in the police department matters little, providing it accomplishes results and the Ogdensburg police force is removed from the joke class. As the force is constituted today, there are several young men, who with proper training, would develop into fine officers, but never under present conditions.

The wibble-wabble way Mayor Lynch and the Common Council, and for that matter, previous mayors, and common councils, have handled police department matters, have been of a laughable character. None of them have shown the least particle of courage and backbone but have allowed things to drift along for many years.

From the government's point of view the supreme issue of the fight is the slip-shod manner previous mayors and common councils have handled police department matters, have been of a laughable character. None of them have shown the least amount of courage and backbone but have allowed things to drift along rather than to take a fearless position for the upbuilding of the force and for the honor of the city.

It has taken a courageous district attorney to take the first step toward bringing order out of chaos in Ogdensburg's police affairs. (While this shake-up business is going on, it might be well if the Republican members of the Council would learn a lesson from District Attorney Ingram in courage and fearlessness, sufficiently enough to make a demand of Mayor Lynch for a division of the city patronage. It is a 50-50 proposition. For a year now Mayor Lynch has been the chief executive of this city and in that length of time he has done nothing toward giving the Republican members their share of the patronage but has on the other hand has antagonized them in every way possible.

The time has now come for the Republican members of the council to demand from the mayor their share of the patronage (political appointments) and at the same time let it be known to him that they are serious.

Under the provisions of the city charter, Mayor Lynch can do nothing without the council. The Republicans should refuse to act on any of his recommendations if the mayor continues to disregard their wishes. City Republicans will stand behind their aldermen. It certainly is time for them to act in this matter and thereby help to build up the (Republican) party in the city. The mayor should study the career of Alfred E. Smith while he was the Democratic governor of this state and learn how beautifully he and a Republican legislature succeeded in their relations with each other. District Attorney William D. Ingram has surely started something.

WHAT MOTIVE BEHIND DA'S THREAT TO INDICT POLICE CHIEF?

Ogdensburg Advance and St. Lawrence Weekly Democrat Editor George Darrow came to the defense of the city's police chief, questioning the motives of the District Attorney in the Oct. 20th edition.

Mayor Lynch said that if the DA had any evidence of the Police

Chief committing a crime, he should present the evidence to the Grand Jury and indict him rather than making threats that he must resign or face charges.

"John D. McCormick is known to everyone as a good, honest, upright citizen, respected by all, and the threat of the district attorney will not injure him in the estimation of the people of the city or the town of Oswegatchie.

The police chief chose not to resign.

Downtown Massena in 1908 (Public Domain)

CHAPTER 6

MASSENA VOTES TO DEFUND VILLAGE POLICE

MASSENA - By the winter of 1921, people across the North Country were unanimous that one municipal police force had repeatedly demonstrated that they were a force to be reckoned with in the war against bootlegging, smuggling and illegal speakeasy enterprises.

Newspapers editors and civic leaders across the state spoke in admiring tones about how the Massena Village Police Department had emerged as modern-day warriors and champions against the illegal forces that insisted on continuing the illegal traffic in booze.

Every day, newspapers across the state reported how Massena police were involved in high-speed chases through the streets of their community to bring the evil doers to justice.

That is why those many admirers were shocked when they learned the residents of Massena overwhelmingly voted in March of 1921 to defend their police force.

Officially, it was not a vote on whether to have a police force. But in March of 1921, when Massena residents went to the polls to vote on portions of the village budget, they sent a clear message that sent shock waves across the state.

The police fund was defeated by an overwhelming vote of 176 to 121.

A year and three months after the United States 18th Amendment had ushered in Prohibition, a majority of Massena voters let it be known at the polls they were fed up with their police department's very successful campaign to put an end to the bootlegging, smuggling and speakeasy enterprises that were helping to put food on the table for many struggling families.

Since the Volstead Act had passed, a growing number of Massena residents had been arrested for violations, ranging from smuggling booze across the border from Canada, transporting liquor downstate or providing alcohol to local buyers.

With the St. Regis Mohawk Reservation sprawling across both sides of the international border, a growing number of Massena residents were making big money by partnering with Mohawks, some of whom had never recognized the international border, much less the U.S. Prohibition Amendment and Volstead laws.

Despite Massena Police Chief Benjamin J. Demo's concerted effort to drive demon rum from Massena's homes and streets, a number of families were growing disenchanted as high-speed chases, gunfights between officers and fleeing vehicles, and searches and seizures became almost daily occurrences.

With state police and federal agents joining Massena police on raids, and federal judges seizing vehicles and issuing fines of $1,000 for possession of alcohol for first-time offenders, the public was discovering that America's "Great Experiment" with alcohol Prohibition was not as simple as the Temperance speakers had once promised.

Village residents showed they were fed up with the police department in March when a majority of voters cast their ballots against the police department's budget in the annual vote during the municipal election.

The police fund was defeated by a vote of 176 to 121.

The voters also defeated a proposition to create a police justice.

The Massena Observer blamed the bootleggers, smugglers, and their supporters for the embarrassing municipal election result.

"Tuesday's village election again demonstrated that people will do some very foolish things without regard to consequences," the newspaper wrote. "The voting down of the appropriations for police, city engineer and the storm water sewer on Main Street are examples. The police fund was beaten by a vote of 176 to 121 and the fund to pay the salary of the city engineer was defeated by the same vote. The proposition to borrow $4,000 to build a drain on Main Street near Joseph Romeo's property was defeated by a vote of 152 to 138.

"Regarding the police fund, it is charged that the bootleggers succeeded in organizing enough opposition to this proposition to defeat it, assisted by other innocent, but misguided, taxpayers who did not take the trouble to find out the real facts in this case."

"The bootleggers, of which Massena has a small army, including sympathizers, have found things getting too warm for them in Massena," the Observer wrote. "It is conceded that Massena has the most efficient police force of any village or city in this section and the bootleggers have found that it is not easy to do business here. Chief Demo has had an offer of $200 per month from another village, which recognizes his worth and it is conceded that he is the best police chief in this north country. Do these friends who so innocently and successfully played into the hands of the criminal class feel proud of the victory they have won?"

Despite the clear public rejection of Massena's campaign to uphold the national prohibition movement, the Observer argued that the majority vote cast by the community's residents needed to be ignored.

"Of course, the police force cannot be disbanded, for some means must be provided to keep it going, but the village board will be greatly embarrassed," the Observer wrote. "The money must come, and the people must pay it. The turning down of the village engineer fund was another instance of propaganda from irresponsible sources, who did not know the value of this official to the village and that his salary is really a saving to the community. Mr. Stevens will be retained, and his salary taken from the general fund and street fund. The turning down of the proposition to raise $4,000 for a stormwater sewer on Main Street near Joseph Romeo's property will lead to a damage suit against the village unless the sewer is built. Mr. Romeo's property is irreparably damaged by flooding at certain times, and he has a legitimate claim. He has not brought a suit because the village officials promised to remedy the situation this summer. If the village must pay heavy damages because of the foolish action of uninformed voters, who is to blame? The sewer will have to be built at any rate.

The Massena Observer conceded that despite their misguided decision on some issues, the residents of the community had supported many beneficial items in the budget.

The propositions for $8,500 for the general fund, $8,000 for the street fund, $6,000 for the fire fund, $6,500 for the light fund, $2,500 for the water fund, $10,759 for the bond and interest fund, $1,500 for the garbage disposal fund, $4,000 for drainage across the high school property, $1,000 for the Howard street sewer fund were all carried by majorities ranging from 9 to 121 votes.

- 79 people voted against paying the bonds and interest due this year on village obligations already incurred.
- 109 people voted against the general fund,
- 8 voted against any money to be used to repair streets,
- 65 voted against having any fire protection,
- 57 voted against lighting the village streets,
- 59 voted against maintaining the water system.

"What can be the state of mind of people who will go to the polls and cast votes against propositions of this kind?" the newspaper asked. "Any community is better off without this class of people. The proposition to pave South Main Street was carried by a majority of only 43, there being 126 votes against it, and the proposition to build a drain so that the high school property can be improved was carried by a majority of only 9.

The proposition to sell the lot on East Orvis Street to Mrs. Oubley was carried by a vote of 223 to 70 and the proposition providing for a police justice was defeated by a vote of 180 to 111.

Massena Newspaper Offers $200 Reward for Information on Crooked Police Officers

A week later, The Massena Observer challenged anonymous critics of the Massena Police force to come forward with any evidence of criminal activity by members of the police force with a front-page advertisement offering a reward:

$200 REWARD

The Massena Observer has received an anonymous communication from one who signs himself "A Respectable Taxpayer." While as a rule we pay no attention to anonymous communications, this one is of interest in view of the action of the voters at the recent village election on the police appropriation.

This anonymous correspondent says: "I am a taxpayer of Massena village and not a bootlegger, but I think it is high time we had a cleaning up of police if we expect to clean up the bootleggers. I can bring a lot of good people who can prove this to you. Go out around and what do you hear?

Massena is the worst place on the map.' Why? " There has been so much talk of late about Massena's police force that the Observer will give a $100 reward, and Village President W. L. Pratt will give another $100 reward for evidence that will prove that any member of the present police force of Massena village is or has been since being on the police force, engaged in assisting in bootlegging, or in aiding or abetting the bootleggers in their work.

No one came forward to collect the reward which was substantial in 1921 with $200 worth about $3,200.

Massena restored its police force funding.

Map Of Canton (Public Domain)

CHAPTER 7

FED THREATENS TO SHOOT CANTON POLICE OFFICER, PUT IN JAIL

FEDERAL DRY AGENT JAILED IN CANTON; PROHIBITION OFFICER LOCKED UP AFTER FIRING 5 SHOTS AT TAXI, FEDERAL AGENT MICHAEL J. C. PHILLIPS, WHO HAS BEEN OPERATING IN OGDENSBURG, HELD FOR HEARING ON CHARGE OF ASSAULT IN FIRST DEGREE - REFUSED TO ACCOMPANY CONSTABLE, SAID TO HAVE THREATENED TO SHOOT HIM — COUNTY SEAT IN TURMOIL

CANTON - Michael J. C. Phillips, one of the federal enforcement agents who have been working in Ogdensburg the past three weeks, was arrested in Canton last night and locked up pending a hearing today on a charge of assault in the first degree. The federal prohibition enforcement agent is accused of firing five shots at a car driven by Ben Hosley, a local taxi man. Hosley swore out a warrant for the arrest of Phillips.

Constable Sanford Jewett said that when he went to arrest Phillips, the federal agent pulled out his revolver and threatened to blow his head off.

Jewett went back with the warrant which was then placed in

the hands of Chief of Police John Devlin, a uniformed officer, who hunted up Phillips, placed him under arrest, and took him before Justice of the Peace Charles M. Hale, who had issued the "warrant."

Judge Hale held the agent for further hearing today and he was committed to jail for the night. During the preliminary examination, Phillips admitted, it is alleged, that he shot at Hosley's car, and that the federal agent refused to accompany the constable who sought to arrest him.

In justification of his actions, Phillips argued he was a federal officer, and his actions were within his rights under his duties to enforce the federal Prohibition laws. Reports reaching here last night from Canton stated that Agent Phillips was standing on the sidewalk when he fired the shots at the taxi. Hosley claims he did not hear the gunshots; it is said and was unaware of what had happened until sometime later when a citizen who witnessed the affair asked him if he had been hurt.

Upon being informed of what occurred, an angry Hosley promptly swore out a warrant for the arrest of the federal officer. The affair caused intense excitement in the county seat last night and much indignation was expressed over what was described as the "wild west" methods employed by the federal officer.

It was said that promiscuous halting and shooting at cars, such as has been going on unhindered in Ogdensburg the past few weeks, would not be tolerated in Canton if there was any way in which it could be stopped, and the action of the taxi driver in promptly seeking legal redress was commended by numerous citizens.

It was predicted last night that the arrest of the federal officer will result in a showdown on the point of whether the federal enforcement agents have any right to halt and search cars without having search warrants.

United States Commissioner Myron Gray of Ogdensburg has

ruled that law enforcement can fire at vehicles that attempt to flee, according to his interpretation of the Volstead Act.

During their operations in Ogdensburg, the enforcement agents halted many cars, but no arrests were made and so far, as could be learned, the officers found no liquor. The federal agents departed from the city a few days ago but it has since been reported that others took their places and that the same methods are still being pursued.

NEW CHARGE MADE AGAINST ENFORCER BY TAXI DRIVER, FEDERAL PROHIBITION AGENT WILL BE ARRAIGNED TODAY FOR RESISTING CANTON CONSTABLE, FIRST CASE TRANSFERRED

CANTON - A second charge, that of resisting an officer who sought to arrest him, was lodged against federal Prohibition Enforcement Agent Michael J. C. Phillips here yesterday after he had been paroled in the custody of U.S. Attorney Dennis B. Lucey on a charge of assault in the first degree, preferred against him by Ben Hosley, a Canton taxi driver. Phillips was rearrested here late in the afternoon by Sheriff Fishbeck of Canton and taken back to the county seat to answer the new second charge.

The arrests grew out of the firing of shots by Phillips when he sought to stop Hosley as he was driving his car through the streets of Canton Thursday night. U.S. Attorney Lucey went to Canton yesterday to appear for Phillips when he was arraigned before Canton Village Judge Charles M. Hale on the charge of assault.

In pursuance of Section 33 of the federal judicial code, U.S. Attorney Lucey requested the case be transferred to the federal courts, which was done. This section provides that a federal officer has the right to have the case removed to the federal courts when a charge is made against him in connection with the performance of his duties.

At the time Constable Jewett of Canton sought to arrest Phillips on the assault charge, it is claimed that he refused to accompany the officer. This formed the basis of the charge of resistance upon which a second warrant was issued yesterday by Justice of the Peace Leon Crary of Canton. This case will come up today before Justice Crary.

District Attorney William D. Ingram of St. Lawrence County will be present to represent the people. Phillips accompanied U.S. Attorney Lucey back to this city following the hearing before Judge Hale on the assault charge. Phillips claims he was acting within his rights as a federal officer, and he did not seem to be disturbed over the charge lodged against him in Canton.

U.S. Attorney Lucey, the top federal prosecutor in upstate New York, whose authority stretched from Binghamton to Plattsburgh had no comment to make regarding the affair. It is understood that Agent Phillips had received a tip that a "booze car" was scheduled to pass through Canton Thursday evening. He posted himself at a point where he expected the machine to pass. When he saw the car, which proved to be a taxi approach, it was said he went out into the road and waved his arms, but the driver kept on. Phillips there upon fired several shots in the air with his revolver.

The cases were transferred to the federal courts where the charges against the agent were dismissed with the federal courts upholding that the federal agents could fire their weapons at anyone who refuses to pull over when officers attempt to search their vehicle.

HUNTING PARTIES IN MALONE SEARCH FOR "WILD MAN"

MALONE - Another cluster of sightings occurred during autumn of 1921, when residents living near Malone organized hunting parties to track down a "wild man." Most of the reports were centered near the hamlet of Skerry, 12 miles to the southwest. A reporter for the *Dunkirk Evening Observer* described the tension in the area: "Women sleep ill o' nights, children are kept from school or guarded by adults on their way there and back, lonely females cower behind locked doors and men wag their heads in gossip as they ponder over the puzzle of the wild man."[27]

Skeptical authorities in Franklin County considered the story unlikely, instead opting to believe that it was "a clever ruse by bootleggers to take advantage of the absence of officers," so they could more easily smuggle liquor across the Canadian border with ease.

CUSTOMS OFFICERS SEIZE 20 BARRELS AND 95 CASES

FOUND IN TRAIN CAR OF POTATOES
Shipment Was Enroute from Montreal to a Firm in Luzerne, Pa., Billed as "Tubers" Value of Contraband Placed at About $25,000 at Canadian Prices; Prominent Montreal Society Woman Arrested at Rouses Point for Smuggling Liquor

OGDENSBURG - Twenty barrels of brandy and 95 cases of whiskey were found secreted in a carload of potatoes which was shipped across the river here yesterday en route from Montreal to Luzerne, Pa. The shipment was billed as potatoes and was consigned to "N. Brown & Co.," of Luzerne by a Montreal firm, according to the customs officers, who made the find while inspecting the contents of the car.[28]

---

[27] Dunkirk Evening Observer, Oct. 22, 1921
[28] Ogdensburg Republican Journal, March 11, 1921

In poking among the potatoes, the inspectors encountered a hard substance which aroused their suspicions and when the potatoes were cleared away the barrels were discovered. The brandy was in "glass bottles carefully packed in the barrels. The car was found to contain 325 bags of potatoes. The liquor and potatoes were seized and removed to the U.S. Customs house on State Street, where they will be kept until disposed of. Their value was not stated by the customs officers but according to current Canadian prices the liquors are worth between $20,000 and $25,000." In as much as potato cars crossing the border are often used to secrete shipments of liquor, custom's officials are on the alert. Inspections are carried out and the vigilance has resulted in seizures being made on numerous occasions.

The discovery was made yesterday by Deputy Collector M. E. Rutherford who immediately notified Collector Henry Holland. A guard was thrown about the car, and no one was permitted to go near it until the liquor had been removed. This was said to be the largest liquor seizure made in Ogdensburg since the Volstead act became operative.

At the U.S. Customs house last night, it was said that potatoes, being perishable, would be sold within a brief time to the highest bidder.

Society Woman Arrested.

Collector Holland yesterday announced that Mrs. Kenneth R. Otis, said to be prominent in social circles in Montreal, was arrested at Rouses Point on Wednesday by Deputy Collector George Warner on a charge of smuggling liquor.

She was taken before United States Commissioner Gilliland at Plattsburgh and held for the action of the grand jury under $500 bail. Mrs. Otis has a summer home at Rouses Point and is well known there. Her husband, who was an engineer officer in the Canadian army, was killed in France, and according to the customs officials she was engaged to marry Major Scott of Montreal on May 18th.

The customs agent stated that Mrs. Otis has been under suspicion in connection with smuggling operations for several months. It is alleged that the customs officials found a large quantity of liquor in the seat which Mrs. Otis occupied in a Pullman car.

The customs officers at Rouses Point also seized a Dodge car containing sixty bottles of liquor yesterday and a few days ago bottles of liquor were found in a car of potatoes that crossed at the same place.

CUSTOMS AGENT HACKMEISTER SEIZES CADILLAC ROADSTER, 20 CASES OF WHISKEY FROM UTICA SMUGGLING PAIR

A Cadillac roadster holding 20 cases of Scotch whiskey and driven by Fred Smith and Harry Bennett of Utica, was seized on the state road between Canton and Potsdam late yesterday afternoon by Federal Agent Ralph E. Hackmeister. [29]

The goods were brought to the local custom house and the men charged with a crime before United States Commissioner Myron B. Gray on a charge of violating Section 33 of the National Prohibition Act. The men gave bail of $500 each and the case was set down for a hearing on December 13th at 2 p.m.

Agent Hackmeister, who works in Northern New York, the nest of bootleggers, is proving to be a terror to smugglers. He is a fearless operator and has averaged a seizure a day for several months. He is rapidly becoming known as one of the most efficient agents in the service and his name brings fear to the Heart of the bootleggers.

---

[29] Ogdensburg Republican Journal, Dec. 5, 1921

Customs Agent in Running, High Speed Gun Battle with Italian Smugglers

Captured Near Potsdam Tony Morra and Philip Fasolo, Italians from Little Falls, were charged with a crime before U.S. Commissioner Gray Saturday morning on a charge of violating the Volstead Act for smuggling liquor. They were represented by R. S. Waterman and were held on $500 bail each for examination.[30]

They were arrested near Potsdam at 1 a.m. Saturday by Customs Agent Ralph Hackmeister after a chase of four miles during which one of the smugglers is alleged to have fired two shots at the Customs officer's car. One of the smuggler's bullets went through a fender and the other punctured a tire.

Agent Hackmeister succeeded in forcing them into the ditch; and the smugglers were obliged to stop. Their car and its contents were seized.

---

[30] Ogdensburg Republican Journal, Dec. 5, 1921

Library and Town Hall, Massena, N. Y.

MASSENA TOWN HALL (AUTHOR'S COLLECTION)

CHAPTER 8

FAMOUS INTERNATIONAL OPIUM SMUGGLER HARRY STONE ARRESTED IN MASSENA IN 1921, LATER KILLED IN FAMOUS MAFIA GUN BATTLE DURING MONTREAL'S BIGGEST BANK ROBBERY

MASSENA - The Massena jail has housed thousands of criminals of all kinds, but the most famous was the notorious international opium smuggler and bank robber Harry Stone, who finally met his death in 1924 in a gun battle after he joined forces with a notorious Canadian Mafia gang to rob Montreal's Bank of Hochelaga.

Three years before his death, Stone made international headlines when he was arrested smuggling opium (worth $2 Million today) across the border into the U.S. through Massena.

Stone was already well known as an international crook and narcotics smuggler when he was arrested by a famous Ogdensburg U.S. Customs Agent on a Canadian National train in Massena on April 6, 1921, with thousands of dollars of drugs in his possession.

He had just arrived from Quebec. U.S. Customs officers had been tipped off that Stone was leaving Montreal with a shipment of narcotics, heading to Massena.

A deputy Customs officer, A.B. Harmon of Malone boarded the train at Huntingdon, Quebec. He had no difficulty identifying his man as the tip of the little finger of Stone's right hand was missing. It was said to have been shot off in a gun fight with officers during a previous arrest.

The officer also found that Stone had a large wardrobe trunk in the baggage car, three suitcases and two handbags. The trunk was bonded and sealed and so was protected from the U.S. Customs Inspector at Fort Covington.

Harmon was instructed not to attempt to molest Stone on the train for fear that innocent civilians might be endangered if Stone began a gunfight to avoid arrest.

The federal officer was instructed to wait until the train reached Massena where Ogdensburg's famous Customs Special Inspector Silas W. Day was waiting to arrest the smuggler and help take him into custody.

Inspector Day was assisted by Massena Police Officer Ivan R. Denison. After the train arrived in Massena, Stone went to the baggage car. Harmon and Day trailed him there. Officer Denison was in uniform and kept out of sight, fearing to alarm Stone.

The drug smuggler was sitting on a box behind the baggage car door. The officers asked him where he was going.

"Here," replied Stone. Under questioning, he admitted he was sometimes known as Harry Stone and when shown his photograph admitted his identity. He was searched, his papers and an automatic revolver were taken from him. It was then that he tried to bribe the officers to let him go.

The officers refused the bribe attempt.

Denison was called in. Stone was handcuffed and taken to the Massena police station, where he was locked in one of the historic cells. An inventory of his baggage disclosed 2,412 ounces of opium and other narcotics of various kinds, including 1,190 ounces of smoking opium and 1,200 ounces of morphine and cocaine.

Fearing that some of Stone's friends might attempt to break into the Massena police station to free him, arrangements were made to have Constable Alonzo A. Riley, armed with a rifle, guard Stone during the night. Riley is still considered one of the best shots in the North Country, although he has only one arm. He was locked in the big cage inside of which the cells are located.

Stone slept but little and talked with the constable much of the time during the night. The smuggler, then but 41 years of age, was of slender build, stoop-shouldered and taller than the average man with sharp features.

Possessed of considerable education and knowing every corner of the globe, he was a fluent talker on almost any subject. Following his arrest here he remained cool and collected. It was characteristic of him. Although unworried over his arrest, he showed considerable concern over the loss of a small notebook containing the names of scores of customers. This was taken from him by the officers.

Stone feared the book might cause trouble to those whose names it contained, scattered all over the world. It would also have been a big asset to him upon his release from jail.

Being in jail was nothing new to him. He laughed when he saw Riley with the rifle. He made no trouble of any kind while in jail.

In a talk with Massena Police Chief Benjamin Demo, he gave an idea as to the value of the drugs seized.

"If those were yours and you knew where to dispose of them, they would bring about $240,000, (about $3.6 million today)" he told the chief with a smile. Stone was arraigned the next morning before United States Commissioner Giles A. Chase and held for the federal grand jury on $825,000 bail, the largest ever fixed by the commissioner. Then he was taken to the county jail at Canton.

Smoking opium is said to be worth $35 a pound to buy, and morphine is worth $22 an ounce. Stone said he valued the lot at $35,000, but that it would sell for much more than that amount.

The dope was all turned over to the federal officers at Ogdensburg who stored it inside the Ogdensburg Post Office and U.S. Customs House on State Street.

According to the government officials, Stone is a native of Chicago. He is 41 years of age and a carpenter by trade. He was previously arrested at San Jose, Calif., and San Francisco under the name of Conrad Johnson on a charge of smuggling narcotics.

The government officers say that Stone is known throughout the country in the illicit drug trade and that his arrest is the most important that has been made on the northern border in many years. The seizure of drugs is likewise the largest ever made in this section.

Three years later, Stone teamed up with members of Montreal's Mafia to rob armed couriers working for Quebec's Bank of Hochelaga to steal $240,000 (worth $3.7 million) they were transporting from branches to the main downtown bank. It was the biggest bank robbery in the history of Canada at the time.

The gangsters arranged to block a tunnel in Montreal where they began a gun battle with the armed guards who were hauling the money in a vehicle.

Stone died during the shootout, along with a bank employee.

One of the Mafia members, Frank Gambino, was related to New York City's Gambino family. He and three other conspirators were later executed for their role in the heist.

One of the gangsters, Adam Parillo, another American, agreed to testify against his accomplices to avoid the death penalty.

He testified that the group had agreed to kick back 10 percent of whatever they stole to Montreal's Mafia boss, Tony "The King" Frank, in exchange for his personal promise that he would use his influence with law enforcement and Quebec's judges to protect them from arrest and prosecution. Parillo received a reduced sentence of 12 years in prison. Morel was given the death penalty for his role in the conspiracy.

But after Parillo was released from the Quebec prison, he was gunned down in Saratoga Springs, New York (a notorious mob hangout during prohibition) in a clear message to anyone who dared to testify against the Mafia. [31]

April 28, 1921, Massena Observer

MASSENA BOOZE MAKING
OUTFIT FOUND IN CELLAR AT DOMINICK ROMEO'S TWO COPPER BOILERS, COPPER WORM, THREE BARRELS OF WHEAT MASH, ALSO, SIX GALLONS OF GRAIN ALCOHOL

MASSENA - Officer Nathan S. Defoy discovered a very complete distillery in the cellar of a house occupied by Dominick Romeo on Woodland Avenue last Saturday while searching for articles alleged to have been stolen from a neighbor. [32]

A search warrant was secured from County Judge Crapser and Officers Defoy, Alguire, and Denison, under the direction of Chief Benjamin Demo, made a seizure Monday afternoon. In the cellar they found two copper boilers: a copper worm and the necessary equipment for making "moonshine," and three barrels of sour wheat mash ready for distilling. One of the copper boilers was made to fit on an oil stove and the other was used on a coal stove. They also found six-gallon bottles of grain alcohol.

---

[31] The Post Star, Glens Falls, N.Y. Dec. 10, 1936
[32] Massena Observer, April 28, 1921

The whole outfit, including liquor, was brought to police head-quarters, and stored in the town hall. Romeo was not at home at the time of the search and seizure.

And he has not yet returned.

The people in that section say that Romeo has been engaged in. this business for some time. Officer Defoy also discovered that liquor was kept in a house at 18 Cornell Avenue, occupied by Joe Kocis. A search warrant was secured, and a search of the premises uncovered 42 quarts of Holland gin, which was hidden under the floor upstairs. The seizure was made by Officers Denison, Alguire, Defoy and LaBrake. Kocis is employed in one of the pot rooms at the Aluminum plant and he was arrested and charged with violating the Volstead law. Kocis gave bail in $1,000 and the examination will be held today

PRESBYTERIAN CHURCH WESTVILLE N.Y. 41.

WESTVILLE, N.Y. ENJOYED A COLORFUL HISTORY DURING THE PROHIBITION ERA BECAUSE IT WAS SO CLOSE TO THE CANADIAN BORDER. (PUBLIC DOMAIN)

CHAPTER 9

America's Most Famous Illegal Speakeasy Operated In Westville, N.Y., Owner Thumbed His Nose at Federal Agents with Bar Stretching Across U.S.- Canada Border

MALONE - April 15 - Notorious bootlegger Joe (Nesit) Castiget enjoyed a colorful career smuggling booze and serving customers at his famous international speakeasy which once straddled the U.S. — Canada border line.[33]

They could confiscate whatever booze they found on the Franklin County side of the speakeasy, but as soon as they left and the coast was clear, he would open back up for business, quenching the thirst of his customers from both sides of the border.

Located on the international boundary line, Castiget frustrated U.S. officials and even Canadian officials with his infamous business that was located partly in Westville, New York and partly on the Canadian side of the line.

Federal officials claimed Castiget had found an innovative way to avoid arrest by locating his illegal business in a building that straddled

---

[33] Massena Observer, April 21, 1921

the border. By sitting on the Canadian side of his speakeasy when U.S. officials attempted to raid his operation from the American side, he could thumb his nose at the frustrated Prohibition agents who had no authority if he stayed on the Canadian side of the building.

If he stayed just out of reach on the Canadian side of his infamous roadhouse, U.S. agents could not arrest him or take him into custody.

Castiget's ingenious strategy made him a legendary figure in the annals of North Country bootleggers and speakeasy operators since his international business taunted local, state, and federal officials in their efforts to shut him down.

His international fame for frustrating both U.S. and Canadian officials eventually led to his undoing when officials from both nations decided to join forces to shut him down by raiding his business simultaneously from both sides of the border.

On April 14, 1921, American officials showed Castiget that even he was not beyond the reach of the international forces of law and order when they were able to team up with Canadian officials who joined them in a coordinated raid on the infamous border operation.

The Massena Observer reported "Malone officials on Wednesday night at about 11 made a successful raid at the notorious line resort of Nesit (Joe) Castignet, the American side of which is in the town of Westville, N.Y.

"The officials seized 60 cases of liquor consisting of various brands of whiskey and gin, the booze being found in the basement of the building on the American side of the boundary line. Officials making the raid include Deputy Customs Collector George F, Cowan, Sheriff Steenberge, Customs Officers Harmon, Stark and Nisbeth, with other assistants.

"Canadian Customs Officer Watson and Inland Revenue Collector McNaughton of Canada, also participated from the Canadian side of the boundary,

"When the "big stock of liquor was seized by the Malone officials, Castignet was in that part of his premises on the Canadian side and for that reason the United States officers could not arrest him.

"Joe, who is an expert in dodging government 'officials, was also safe from arrest by the Canadian officers, as they have no power of arrest under the provisions of the Canadian statute. The seized liquors were brought to Malone by the local officials, but as of noon yesterday the inventory had not been made. It is believed, however, that the estimate of 270 quarts is below, rather than above, the count. The value is upwards of $8,500 (worth over $125,000 today) based on the price received by the bootlegger. With several large seizures of liquors made in the Malone area within the past few days, Customs officials believe bootleggers are facing an acute shortage due to the success of the federal crackdown.

DETROIT'S NOTORIOUS PURPLE GANG (WIKIMEDIA COMMONS)

CHAPTER 10

BROOKLYN MOBSTER'S CAREER GOT START SMUGGLING BOOZE BY LEASING MADRID PLANT TO MAKE COTTAGE CHEESE

MADRID - Brooklyn mobster Samuel Adamson's criminal career started when he escaped St. Lawrence County Sheriff's Deputies by fleeing out the back door of a Madrid cheese factory but ended eight years later in a Detroit restaurant in a hail of bullets fired by a notorious professional assassin.

For Adamson, the son of Jewish immigrants, the mob and organized crime in the 1920s provided a way to make a living at a time when his religion and Eastern European ethnic background made him the target of discrimination.

It also led him to start his criminal career by coming to a small town called Madrid, New York in St. Lawrence County where he and his criminal associates in Brooklyn believed they could make big money, lured by their belief that the rural law enforcement authorities in Northern New York would never discover their criminal smuggling operation.[34]

---

[34] Ogdensburg Republican Journal, April 11, 1921

Adamson, like many Jewish youngsters in 1920's Brooklyn, faced rampant antisemitism which barred him, his family, and friends from many employment opportunities, helping to encourage an environment in Brooklyn's Jewish ghettos where some immigrant children found they needed to be quick with their fists and willing to turn to a life of crime to get their piece of the American dream they'd heard so much about.

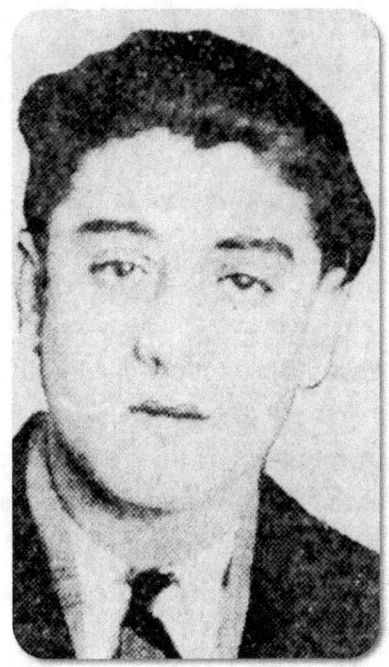

IRVING SHAPIRO, NOTORIOUS DETROIT HITMAN
CHIEF SUSPECT IN SAMUEL ABRAMSON'S ASSASSINATION

While the vast majority of Jewish youngsters worked hard, struggling to succeed despite the many obstacles they found in their path in the U.S., a few young immigrants, and children of immigrants of all nationalities turned to crime, especially as Prohibition opened a new pathway to riches they could have only dreamed about.

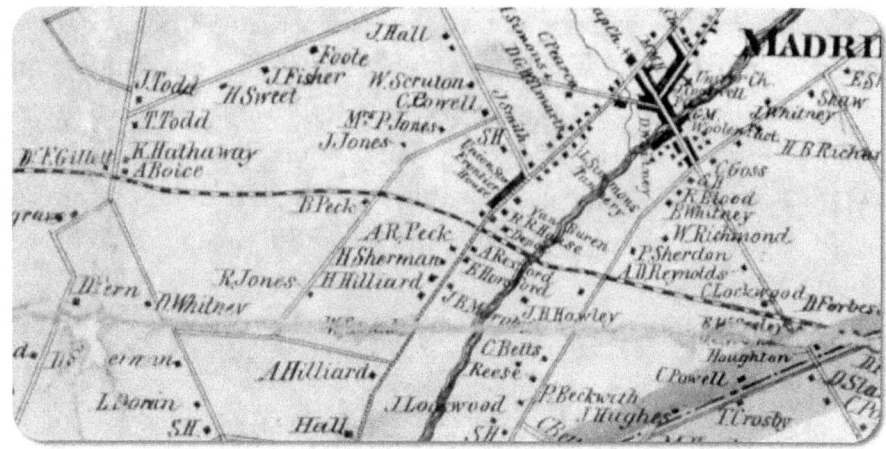

MADRID SEEMED LIKE THE PERFECT PLACE FOR THE BROOKLYN MOB

It also sometimes offered a way of life that for some eventually led to an early and violent death.

When Abramson was eventually murdered, police found his body in a dirty alleyway.

Police detectives had little doubt who committed the bloody murder.

They confided to reporters at the Detroit Free Press in the July 29, 1929, edition that they suspected a professional hitman, the notorious gunman and mob assassin Irving Shapiro, fired the shots that took Abramson's life in a downtown Detroit restaurant and then disposed of his body in the alley.[35]

Police described Abramson's high profile murder as part of what could be expected among those who, like Abramson, chose to move from Brooklyn to join the colorful Detroit Purple Gang, a group of violent Jewish mobsters who supplied liquor to Chicago's Al Capone gang and whose members were suspected by some historians of serv-

_____
[35] Detroit Free Press, July 29, 1921

ing as the violent hitmen who carried out the grisly Chicago St. Valentine's Day Massacre.

For a Brooklyn gangster like Sam Abramson, Madrid, New York in rural upstate New York in 1921, eight years before his violent murder, must have seemed like a dream come true.

The small hamlet of about 150 families on the banks of the Grasse River, was the kind of quiet rural community where a street wise young man like Abramson must have been convinced, he could operate a criminal smuggling operation without a care in the world.

After all, the tiny town of Madrid did not even have a police force.

The upstate hicks who lived in the area would never figure out what he and his pals were doing right under their noses.

And if they did, what were a bunch of farmers and shopkeepers going to do about it?

With federal prohibition agents prowling the roads across upstate New York, searching vehicles for Canadian liquor, Sam was convinced that he had found the perfect scheme to safely ship Canadian liquor to New York City's thirsty speakeasy patrons.

His secret?

Cottage cheese!

The Brooklyn gangster had come up with what seemed like the perfect get rich quick scheme.

He hired Massena criminals to help smuggle liquor across the St. Lawrence River at night. The smugglers were under orders to haul it to a small cheese plant in Madrid where Abramson and his partner, Benjamin Kissen, packed the bottles of Canadian whiskey in large metal milk canisters. They then topped off the canisters with cottage cheese made at the cheese plant from local milk brought to the plant from nearby Madrid area farms.

With times tough in Madrid and Northern New York, the struggling dairy farmers were more than happy to have a place where they could sell their milk.

The owner of the plant had been more than willing to accept money from a Brooklyn city slicker who offered cash to lease the struggling cheese plant.[36]

MADRID RAILROAD DEPOT (COURTESY MADRID TOWN HISTORIAN)

Abramson saw it as a fool proof way to make money.

The cottage cheese containers would then be shipped by rail to New York City where fellow gang members unloaded the canisters from the freight cars for sale to Brooklyn speakeasies.

Madrid offered a convenient rail depot where the containers could be shipped from.

Abramson hired three Massena criminals, Alfred Baxter, Sylvester Planty and John Vail, to help, attracted by the lure of easy money.

---

[36] Ogdensburg Republican Journal, April 11, 1921

They agreed to lease William Aken's cheese plant as part of the elaborate scheme.

Samuelsen told Aken that he had perfected a "secret technique to make cottage cheese from skim milk" which required him to mix it late at night to protect his recipe.

The gangsters arranged to have the Canadian liquor smuggled across the St. Lawrence River by boat and transported to the Madrid cheese plant where they carefully packed the whiskey inside cans filled with cottage cheese.

METAL MILK CONTAINER (AUTHOR'S COLLECTION)

From the Madrid railroad connection, they could ship it to New York where the Brooklyn mobsters could sell the Canadian whiskey for higher prices than the bathtub gin and homemade beer their competitors were selling to speakeasies and underground saloons.

But Abramson never reckoned that the St. Lawrence County Sheriff's Department and Assistant District Attorney would soon be hot on his trail.

On April 13, the Potsdam Courier reported that Sheriff's Deputy S. R. Lockwood and his associates organized a late-night raid on the illegal operation.[37]

Deputy Lockwood had grown suspicious about the Madrid cheese plant ever since he heard men from Brooklyn were leasing the plant. The explanation that they needed to make cottage cheese at night to protect their "trade secrets" seemed a little too far-fetched for the deputy to believe.

Assistant St. Lawrence County District Attorney Andrew Hanmer had tried to enlist the aid of St. Lawrence County Sheriff Lawrence Fishbeck to lead the raid on the Brooklyn mob's cheese plant.

But when he found the Sheriff was out of town, he directed Deputy Sheriff Lockwood to round up a group of officers to conduct the raid.

Deputy Sheriff Lockwood and his assistants concealed themselves near the factory and waited. At about 10:30 p.m. under the cover of darkness, they watched as a car arrived and men began unloading its contents and taking them into the cheese plant.

The officers watched as the men began to unload the liquor and then they sprung their carefully laid trap on the occupants. In the car were Baxter, Planty and John Vail.

Waiting for them inside the factory were the two Brooklyn men, Abramson and Kissen. They came out of the factory to help unload the car.

When the police announced themselves in the darkness, Baxter, the driver of the vehicle, tried to start the engine.

---

[37] Potsdam Courier, April 13, 1921

The officers, however, drew their revolvers and ordered him to throw up his hands, which he did. They then placed handcuffs on him.

While this was going on, two men escaped. Planty and Kissen were later arrested on the streets of Madrid village.

Abramson used the confusion caused by Planty and Kissen's escape to flee the scene of the law enforcement raid into the darkness. He escaped without any overcoat. He had been wearing just an undershirt and overalls when the Sheriff's deputy and constables launched the raid.

He ran through the streets of Madrid to escape from the officers, eventually finding a place to hide inside a barn.

While the arrest of Planty and Abramson's partner, Kissen, was being made, Baxter, who had already been handcuffed, jumped from the car, and escaped from the officers.

Baxter also fled through the streets of Madrid, eventually going north where he wandered through a cemetery.

He sawed the handcuff chain on the top of a gravestone in the Madrid cemetery. His wrists were badly cut and bruised when he smashed the cuffs on the same stone to get free from the metal restraints.

He spent the rest of the night walking the 18 miles to Massena, arriving Friday morning, only to be greeted and arrested by Massena Chief of Police B. J. Demo and taken back to Madrid for arraignment.

Meanwhile, when morning dawned, Abramson slipped out of the barn and hired Hugh Arnold to drive him to Massena for $7.

MADRID HOTEL
PRESENT DAY MADRID HOTEL (AUTHOR'S COLLECTION)

The Massena Observer reported in its April 14th edition that Massena Police Officer Denison trailed Abramson to Chase Mills, overtaking him six miles west of Massena.[38]

DOWNTOWN DETROIT
WIKIMEDIA COMMONS

---

[38] Massena Observer, April 14, 1921

With no lockup in Madrid, Deputy Sheriff Lockwood and his men sat up all night in the Madrid hotel office guarding Planty and Kissen until they were able to charge them with a crime in front of Madrid's Justice of the Peace.

A hearing was held there Friday. Attorney Barney F. 0'Neil appeared for the defendants, the arraignment being before Justice of the Peace Edward P. Martin of Madrid. Each waived examination and all were held for the grand jury.

The bootleggers pleaded not guilty, waived examination and were held for the grand jury which met in Canton in May.

The 35 cases of Canadian liquor destined to be shipped inside metal milk containers with cottage cheese to hide their contents were seized and stored in the St. Lawrence County Jail by deputies.

Baxter and Abramson were held on $1,000 bail each and Planty and Kissen on $500 bail each. The Brooklyn gangsters furnished bail.

When they eventually pleaded guilty, St. Lawrence County Judge John Crapser sentenced Abramson and Kissen to pay $500 fines. They quickly left town and headed back to Brooklyn.

With his dreams of cottage cheese riches shattered, Abramson returned to Brooklyn until he was recruited two years later with several other Brooklyn mobsters to move to Detroit where they joined Detroit's notorious "Purple Gang.

The Purple gang was Detroit's most notorious criminal organization in the 1920s and 1930s. Led chiefly by the Burnstein brothers - Raymond, Joseph, Isadore, and Abraham - the Purple Gang was made up of Jewish immigrants who had moved from Brooklyn to Detroit's lower east side.

CHICAGO MOB BOSS AL CAPONE
WIKIMEDIA COMMONS

OLD LOG CABIN WHISKEY
WIKIMEDIA COMMONS

The Brooklyn mobsters soon joined forces with the "Oakland Sugar House Gang," another group of Jewish mobsters who had started out stealing fruit, candy, and other small items from Jewish merchants but eventually graduated to robbing drunks and shaking down Jewish shopkeepers for money.

The arrival of Prohibition convinced the Oakland Sugar House gang composed of Harry Fleisher, Henry Shore, Eddie Fletcher, Irving Milberg, Harry Altman, Harry Keywell, and Morris and Phil Raider that they could make more money by working together with "The Purple Gang" under the leadership of Abe Bernstein to import liquor across the Detroit River from Canada.

For several years, the Purples supplied Canadian whiskey — Old Log Cabin — to Al Capone's organization in Chicago.

PURPLE GANG SMUGGLING IN BOOZE (DETROIT NEWS)
WIKIMEDIA COMMONS

Old Log Cabin was a well-known whiskey brand that was heavily in demand in the speakeasies controlled by the Capone mob in Chicago.

However, when Chicago's Bugs Moran directed his mob to hijack a shipment of Old Log Cabin whiskey from the Detroit criminals, the enraged members of the Purple Gang vowed revenge.

Not long afterwards, seven of Bugs Moran's gangsters were executed in the notorious St. Valentine's Day Massacre in 1929. Chicago police considered the Detroit Purple Gang's mobsters and notorious contract hitman Fred "Killer" Burke their prime suspects but were never able to pin the bloody mass murder on them.

Meanwhile, members of the Purple Gang branched out into more criminal fields to make money. Abramson became a successful bondsperson, putting up bail at extortionate rates to get fellow criminals out of jail.

DETROIT'S NOTORIOUS PURPLE GANG
WIKIMEDIA COMMONS

Others hijacked prizefight films and forced movie theaters to show them for a high fee. Some members defrauded insurance companies by staging fake accidents. Others kidnapped people.

The Purple Gang was Detroit's most notorious organized crime gang during the early days of Prohibition.

But Detroit's Purple Gang became best known as cold-blooded contract killers, a lucrative murder-for-hire business that earned them the respect of fellow hoodlums across the country who employed them for jobs they didn't want to do themselves and felt that bringing someone in from outside would help keep their involvement in the murder a secret from other mobsters and the authorities.

Unfortunately, when the Purple Gang's top leadership - Abe Axler, Eddie Fletcher, Harry Sutton, and Irving Milberg - were sentenced to federal prison at Leavenworth for conspiracy to violate the liquor laws, the organized crime syndicate they had worked so hard to build in the Detroit underworld began to unravel. Abramson's murder by Shapiro was just one of many killings that showed the Purple Gang's reign of terror was unraveling. But Shapiro's decision to kill one of the gang's longtime members soon led to violent revenge.

Shapiro's bloody body was found soon after Abramson's murder by police on the streets of Detroit in what the Detroit Free Press's reporters suspected was retaliation for Abramson's murder by his friends in the Purple Gang who felt the young thug had crossed the line by killing one of their early members. Shapiro was shot to death and his body was dumped close to Abramson's home in what Detroit detectives described as a symbolic gesture by Detroit's Jewish "Kosher Nostra."

DETROIT'S NOTORIOUS PURPLE GANG DOMINATED THE CITY'S HEADLINES

NEW YORK GOVERNOR NATHAN LEWIS MILLER

CHAPTER 11

NEW YORK WINS WAR, STAMPS OUT LIQUOR, GOVERNOR NATHAN MILLER CLAIMED IN 1921

When Republican Governor Nathan Louis Miller ran for New York's top job, he promised to crack down and enforce the new Prohibition law by dramatically expanding the New York State Police in areas like Northern and upstate New York where they could prevent booze from being brought in from Canada.

He also championed the Mullan-Gage Law which spelled out the powers of local law enforcement officers to enforce Prohibition, which also gave police the power to search for alcoholic beverages whenever and wherever they wished. They did not need either probable cause or even a search warrant. This was the strictest of the dry laws in New York State history.

Not long after taking office, he and his administration were boasting about how his crackdown on the illegal liquor trade in Northern New York would soon bring an end to the smuggling, bootlegging and speakeasies that were making a mockery of the 18th amendment.

One of the major steps was stationing a new barracks with an entire state police troop of 58 officers in Malone where troopers could fan out from Franklin County into St. Lawrence and Clinton counties by patrolling the international border with Canada.

North Country Glad to Greet State Police, Believe New Troop Means Booze Running Will Stop — Bootleggers' Worried

MASSENA, Feb. 28.—With the report that a new barracks and troop of the state police is to be placed in the north country, with either Malone or Watertown as headquarters, there has come to light here, a marked feeling that at last bootlegging across the Canadian border will be stopped or at least appreciably checked.[39]

While north country people, interested in seeing the Volstead law enforced, have felt that the authorities who have been working here this winter have done their utmost, there is still a belief that a troop of state police will go a long distance toward bringing about the desired result. Massena citizens today recalled how just before Christmas one lone trooper went into a deserted farmhouse not far away on the road towards Malone and arrested three men there.

The three men paid heavy fines, and the lone police officer brought out 12 cases of whiskey. And these same citizens were jubilant in their belief that if one trooper could do so much, an entire troop could virtually stop bootlegging. The open winter has been an immense help to contraband runners. They have been able to shoot across the border in high-powered cars and during only one night, have been successful in putting more than 100 miles between them and the border patrols. And it is a watchword among bootleggers and whiskey runners that the interior is easy to get through once the border patrols are passed.

Ogdensburg has continually reported wild night riders in cars

---

[39] Massena Observer, Feb. 28, 1921

which boast big engines. These birds have flown through the city "on high" almost every night this winter. To stop them a handful of Federal agents have been on duty. And they have had little chance. Now and then strangers have appeared and for a day or two the rushing of contraband has died down. Because it is perfectly true that the whiskey runners have their own spy system and have "spotted" these strangers, it is equally as true that the agents have had little chance.

In addition, agents have come here and openly confiscated liquor. But when the confiscated beverages get to the testing places in federal buildings, cases have been missing. This situation has given the whole north country uneasy thoughts when it considers bootlegging as a business. People up here have realized and still do realize that the Volstead Act, as far as the Canadian border here is concerned, is not particularly well enforced. Now, with the coming of the state police, they believe things will be different. The state troopers have always had a habit of doing what they start to do, and whiskey runners have already started an undercurrent campaign against having a troop in the section. Massena does not care whether Watertown or Malone is the headquarters. Either place will do as far as Massena and Ogdensburg are concerned. The main idea is that the two towns want the law enforced and "believe the troopers can do it."

TROOPERS LOCATE BARRACKS IN MALONE TO FIGHT BOOTLEGGERS

MALONE - An increase of 100 men in the state police force has been announced. The men will be divided into two troops, one of which is certain to be placed at Malone, and the other to be stationed at Binghamton.

Citizens of Malone will be asked to furnish quarters for the new troops, on the same basis of cost-plus 10 percent that private houses in Oneida, Troy and Batavia are now leased to the state police under a ten-year agreement. Malone opinion holds that the establishment there of the state troopers means the beginning of a stricter watch on whiskey smuggling activities across the Canadian border. Last year state police were stationed in small numbers on the border, but they were too few to efficiently check the widespread bootlegging from Canada.[40]

MALONE TROOPERS TO FIGHT SMUGGLERS

MALONE - Malone would be glad to have a troop of state police located here but not at the expense of the forests, fish, and game interests of Northern New York. The duties of protectors who know the ground and roam the forests on foot cannot be done by troopers on horseback or motorcycles.[41]

And the expense would be greater than before. The chief benefit of a troop here would be to assist county officers in the enforcement of the state prohibition law which is on Governor Miller's program, and the suppression of liquor smuggling over the border.

A whole troop of state police here patrolling our northern roads would be a terror to the bootleggers, for that, Northern New Yorkers would hold up their hands in approval. It is said that Malone will be asked to furnish quarters for the troop on much the same basis that troops are now housed at Oneida, Troy, and Batavia. Buildings are built for the state police and leased to the state based on a ten-year lease, with the privilege reserved to the state for purchase for cost plus 10 percent at the end of this period.

---

[40] Chateaugay Record, March 11, 1921
[41] Malone Farmer, March 21, 1921

Since the announcement of the formation of two new troops was made, we notice that in addition to game protection and the suppression of bootlegging, factory inspection will also be a part of the new duties of the state police and the force of factory inspectors will, of course, be abolished.

The new northern district, as planned, will include Jefferson, St. Lawrence, Lewis, Hamilton, Franklin, Clinton and Essex counties, and the wooded section of Herkimer County.

While Malone has been tentatively selected for the post, Watertown is in the field as a rival, with the claim that that city is the best location. Each of the new troops will have a captain, two lieutenants and 95 men. The proposals for transferring power over game protection will be incorporated in the measure for the increase in the state police force.

Major Chandler, head of the state police, who has decided to withdraw his resignation, is confident that his men will be able to cope with booze smuggling over the border.

With North Country public opinion in the rural communities heavily in favor of the plan to launch a major crack down on the illegal booze runners bringing liquor across the Canadian border into New York State, Governor Miller and his advisors wanted to move forward with their effort to shut off the flow of liquor, even if the new state police troop and barracks were several months from being ready.

They reasoned, if they provided the leadership and brought together the federal, state, county, and local agencies to focus their combined attention on the rumrunners, they could deal a major blow to the illegal networks that were forming and show that New Yorkers were united and ready to stamp out demon rum.

The New York Herald and other newspapers across the state trumpeted the plan to the Empire State's residents to reassure them that the new governor was serious.

NEW YORK HERALD REPORTS MAJOR
CRACKDOWN PLANNED ON BORDER

MALONE - The first serious attempt to stop the flow of Canadian whiskey over the New York State boundary will be planned here tomorrow when Major George F. Chandler, superintendent of the State Police, and the sheriffs, district attorneys, police chiefs and magistrates of the counties of Franklin, St. Lawrence, Clinton, and Essex will confer.[42]

Henry Holland, Collector of Customs for the Northern District, will attend the conference, and the chief topic of discussion will be ways and means of enforcing the new State prohibition laws.

Mr. Holland will defend the erstwhile activities of the Customs Collectors who have borne the burden of what little opposition the rum runners have encountered.

He will show that the greater portion of the liquor smuggled into New York State from Canada comes in by motor cars over the seventy-five miles of frontier between the St. Lawrence River and Lake Champlain.

And along this wide-open frontier is fewer than thirty U.S. Customs officers. Volstead agents have been an uncertain agency along that part of the border, according to the Customs men.

With state police and county officials cooperating with the Government, the business of booze running from Canada will be a much more serious matter to the smugglers. The members of the judiciary attending the meeting will be urged to try jail sentences for first offenders instead of mere fines, which are always paid in cash and joyously.

---

[42] New York Herald, New York City, April 28, 1921

It is planned that state and county police do patrol work in fast automobiles and that the state border be divided into sectors, each of which will be presided over by a certain number of police.

The governor and his advisors gloated as they saw their proposed campaign gaining glowing endorsements from both rural and big city newspapers across the state with the press and public overwhelmingly accepting their argument that a coordinated and concerted campaign directed by Albany with several hundred gray clad troopers on horseback would easily end the scourge posed by the dark scourge of the rumrunners.

Troopers on mighty black steeds vs. gangsters in high-powered, souped-up motor cars.

They reasoned, what could go wrong?

TROOPERS TO END N.Y. LIQUOR RUNNING
FORCE OF 848 HORSEMEN TO BE TURNED
LOOSE ON UPSTATE BOOTLEGGERS

ALBANY, N. Y. - On the final day of July, 848 husky and fearless young New York State Troopers will start out on the trail of bootleggers, rum runners, moonshiners, and the keepers of roadhouses where preprohibitlon joys can still be indulged if one has the price. [43]

They are going to mop up all the moisture in the rural sections of New York State the same as the police are doing in New York City. This statewide drive on the booze carriers was made possible by Governor Miller when he signed the bill increasing the number of

---

[43] Adirondack News, St. Regis Falls, April 30, 1921

State police troops. Governor Miller signed the bill in the presence of Major George P. Chandler, head of the State Police, and the two held a long conference on plans for making life unhappy for prohibition violators. Major Chandler that strong arm methods will be used If necessary to put out of business every illicit rum seller in the rural sections of the state.

"We will do everything in our power to back up Governor Miller in the enforcement of the Mullan-Gage laws and to cooperate with both the federal and local authorities in making the state dry," he said.

To enlist the extra troopers, Major Chandler, anticipating the signing of the bill, has been working night and day in conducting examinations. He is looking for the highest type of young men.

The exams are the most rigid he ever held, so severe, in fact, that not more than one applicant in ten can pass the test. The men must be perfect, physically, clean morally and have a fair education. They must also prove that they are fearless.

With the public's interest in the state cleaning up the rural liquor trade at a fever pitch, the governor and his team decided that they would not wait until they had established the new troops of state police in Malone and downstate. During their 4-county conference that brought together federal, state, county, and local law enforcement in late April, they had mapped out a May surprise for the criminals to put a stop to their successful efforts thumbing their noses at the Prohibition law.

The May 7, 1921, edition of the Adirondack News was just one of numerous newspapers that breathlessly reported Albany claims that the governor's statewide campaign was already turning the tide against the purveyors of demon rum upstate, even though the actual raid occurred just 20 miles north of the New York City borough of the Bronx.

TROOPERS SURPRISE N.Y. RUM RUNNERS
MAJOR CHANDLER OPENS WAR WITHOUT WAITING FOR MORE STATE POLICE

ALBANY — Instead of waiting until his two new troops are recruited and trained, Major George F. Chandler, commanding the state police, started attacking rum runners, bootleggers, and blind tigers.[44]

He changed his plans overnight. It was believed he would defer action until his forces had been enlarged from their present strength to their newly authorized level. That would mean sometime between June 10 and July 1.

The booze runners and consumers were caught unawares.

Due to the extent of the rum running conditions across the New York - Canadian boundary, the major decided to hesitate no longer. Major Chandler began operations by detailing his men to the north country district, where the eighteenth amendment had been flagrantly violated with impunity and where erstwhile efforts to suppress the liquor traffic have been regarded as merely official pleasantries.

Other troopers were assigned to descend on roadhouses that have been an oasis for city folks who were shut off from their liquor by local police raids. The first thing done was a raid on a White Plains place (in Westchester County, just outside New York City), where about $25,000 worth of liquor was captured.

In the meantime, the mayor said he would hustle his recruiting along in order that the additional men appropriated for by the legislature may get into the cleanup fight within the coming month.

---

[44] Adirondack News, St. Regis Falls, May 7, 1921

As soon as a new troop is found fit for service, hard, grueling service, that will require courage and honesty—these new men will be thrown Into the Adirondack district, where the bootleggers have opened their headquarters. Then he intends stationing his men along the 76 miles of open border between Rouses Point and Fort Covington.

With plans moving ahead to expand the state police to combat the forces of rum, Albany officials announced that they had decided what everyone had concluded months before. They would locate their trooper barracks in Malone, not Watertown.

Just as importantly, the new Troop B home of the Grey Riders Black Horse Troop would be outfitted with the latest in technology, even including a telephone to allow the officers to keep in contact with each other as well as other agencies.

In the 1920s, few people owned phones and many of the rural areas where the troopers would patrol on horseback had no phone service available. However, limited phone service was available in many upstate communities as well as most law enforcement agencies.

MALONE TO GET TELEPHONE CONNECTION
WILL BUILD SIXTY THOUSAND DOLLAR TROOPER BARRACKS

Malone was chosen as the headquarters for the new "B" Troop of the State Constabulary when members of the Chamber of Commerce met Major George F. Chandler, commanding officer, at a luncheon in the Elks Club.[45]

In one hour and ten minutes, $60,000 was subscribed for construction of a barracks.

---

[45] Chateaugay Record, May 13, 1921

Merchants were unanimous in their desire to have the troop located there and were enthusiastic when Major Chandler outlined details.

The new troop comprising sixty men and their mounts, as well as families will be brought to Malone June 15.

If the barracks are not completed until after that date, temporary quarters for the men will be at the Smith house. Major Chandler selected these quarters following the meeting.

The usual procedure in constructing the barracks will be applied as it has in other towns where troops are stationed. The state will lease the barracks with an option to buy in ten years, paying ten per cent on the investment, Major Chandler explained.

Establishment of the troop here is taken as an indication that bootlegging activities will soon be stopped.

Beside taking up points regarding the troop, Major Chandler gave a history of the organization and the work it has accomplished since it was formed. He was followed by Dr. Earl A. Bates of Syracuse who also spoke about the troopers. Troopers. Among those present was State Treasurer N. Monroe Marshall whose home is in Malone. On behalf of the People's Trust Company of which he is president, he subscribed $10,000 toward the fund.

Work on the barracks will begin immediately.

As an indication of how seriously the state took its responsibility to provide the state of the art equipment the state police would need to stamp out the Cadillac and Buick driving liquor smugglers, the governor's advisors let it be known that the 58 troopers stationed in Malone would have also have 8 motorcycles while the rest would have thoroughbred horses to patrol the rural roads along the border.

With 30 federal Customs officers helping to monitor the smugglers along the 75 miles along the border, the State Police Commander appeared certain he and his 56-trooper force would soon have the liquor smuggling problem under control.

With bootleggers earning as much as $2,500 a load for many of the shipments they carried and federal fines averaging about $500 for an occasional arrest, the $2,000 (worth $31,000 today) profit margin the rum runners enjoyed (even when they were arrested) offered all the incentive the growing criminal element needed to face off against 30 Customs agents and 58 troopers, most of whom were on horseback.

In 1921, state police began conducting raids and made more than 300 arrests across what Albany described as the "bootlegger strong-holds" of Clinton, Franklin, and St. Lawrence counties. The troopers began with raids on St. Regis, Tupper Lake, Malone, Port Henry and Ausable Forks.

In Tupper Lake, troopers raided nine homes, seizing $6,800 worth of liquor

In Essex County, they seized $3,000.

Over six months, they averaged one raid every five weeks.

With just 60 men to patrol over 7,000 square miles in New York's rugged and rural North Country, the Gray Riders of Troop B battled the growing booze criminal empire that somehow continued growing as more people found that it offered a real get rich quick opportunity for those willing to take a negligible risk.

In 1921, Canada showed its views on Canadians looking to get rich off America's growing thirst for beer, wine, and liquor.

An Ontario judge ruled that Canadian distilleries and breweries could legally produce alcohol despite laws banning its domestic sale if the businesses only sold it for export.

The province of Ontario decided that companies like Seagram's, Bronfman and others could produce as much liquor as they wanted if it was shipped out of Canada and into the hands of bootleggers, smugglers and gangsters who were supplying the thirsty drinkers of the U.S.A.

Both federal and state officials continued to insist that they were turning the tide on the growing criminal enterprise. In fact, by May 20, 1921, Major Chandler and Governor Miller's aides were already declaring victory in their efforts, just five months after the new Governor had taken office.

TRAILS BLOCKED
DISTRICT WILL SOON BE BONE DRY
ACCORDING TO WISE ALBANY NEWS GATHERER

May 20, 1921 - At the end of three weeks of intensive rum fighting by the state troopers, a survey of the liquor enforcement situation in this State under the new Administration reveals these key facts: *"The Adirondack whiskey route from the Canadian distilleries has been broken. The dauntless troopers have driven at least two-thirds of the bootleggers and rum runners from their mountain strongholds in the northern part of the state and dammed this main source of New York city's booze supply.* With their underground mountain connections broken, the bootleggers have established a new chain through Vermont, Massachusetts, and Connecticut to the Hudson River and from concealed nooks and coves along the river are smuggling their wet goods by big and little boats to the New York markets.[46]

The campaign of the State Police force is now centered along the unfrequented highways and the river leading to New York from the Vermont-Connecticut route. The liquor law is being enforced more rigidly in New York city than upstate. Most of the upstate cities have many wet spots.

---

[46] Chateaugay Record, May 27, 1921

Their outside sources of supply are dwindling fast, and they are selling "hootch" which may not kill but certainly does intoxicate.

Gov. Miller's representatives are closely observing the tax enforcement by up-State municipal police. It is likely that the Governor may act soon. Some of the police chiefs of up-State cities may be sent out of jobs before many weeks pass. The rural districts throughout the State are fast approaching a bone-dry condition. Fully one quarter of all the wet spots, like famous roadhouses, have been put out of business in the three-week drive of the troopers. It is predicted by the state police that by July in this State, outside of the cities, will be bone dry.

These facts show how fast this state is moving toward complete dryness. The State Enforcement act, modeled after the Volstead law, has been in actual operation for little more than a month. Yet in that time 50 per cent of the moisture in the State has been mopped up. The task has been fully two-thirds accomplished in three weeks. By July 1, state troopers say, the mountain route will have been abandoned.

With only a handful of men, Major Chandler has driven hundreds of bootleggers out of the mountains. With another hundred troopers available in another month, the task will be completed in short order. Where a dozen to twenty trucks, heavily laden with Canadian rye and Scotch were sneaking through the mountains with lights out in the night hours, paying the graft toll exacted by somebody and getting their illicit and precious cargoes safely to the New York city consumer, there are not now more than two or three "night riders" who get through the lines of State troopers. The troopers have proof that the same gangs of bootleggers who operated through the Adirondacks since the Volstead law became effective have shifted to the Vermont Connecticut route.

They try to get through unfrequented roads in the southern part of the State to the Hudson River or road.

There their loads are distributed and in every conceivable manner are smuggled into New York. The troopers are just beginning to deal with the smuggling into the State down along the lower Hudson. As fast as men become available, they will be sent to posts in that section. It is predicted here that by July 1, fifteen days after the new troop goes on duty, this route will also have been stopped.

Major Chandler has just returned from an inspection tour through the northern part of the State. Following his custom of not discussing his job until things have happened, he declined to give any details, but said he was entirely satisfied with the work of his men up along the border.

The troopers in three weeks have made 290 arrests in the rural districts. The places raided are out of business. Waiters have been dismissed and bars boarded up, the famous drinking places along the Saugerties Road, the wonderful taverns of other days out along the plank road near Syracuse, the roadhouses near Rochester and Buffalo, as well as other places of that class throughout the State are gone.

It is evident that fully one-quarter of the rural drinking resorts have been closed. The troopers now allow themselves one month to finish the job. But in the cities of upstate it is quite a different story.

There is not the slightest doubt that Commissioner Enright has done a better job than any other municipal police official in the state. Municipal administrations have laid down on the job. They don't know it, but they are lying on dynamite.

When Gov. Miller gave notice that he would remove any police official who failed to enforce the law, the upstate police chiefs smiled and remarked that the Governor meant Enright. Nobody upstate would be bothered, they said.

If conditions continue in the upstate cities for another month as they are today there will be an explosion. Any man upstate can get it if he has the price and wants to take the trouble of getting introduced properly to the hootch man.

There are dozens of saloons operating in Albany, Troy, Schenectady, Syracuse, Rochester, Buffalo, and most of the other fifty odd cities.

The smaller the city, the drier it is. This is the situation the Governor's agents are watching. In addition to the saloons where drinks still may be had in the backroom or upstairs if one knows the boss, there are scores and hundreds of speakeasies of the fake clothing store brand, where bad whiskey is hidden in piles of cheap clothing and a friend can get his drink for a dollar.

Major Chandler has just finished recruiting his new troop, and the 120 men, picked from 1,800 applicants, are now in training.

The questionnaires these men had to answer made some of inventor Thomas Edison's exams he gives potential employees look easy. The applicants who wanted to ride one of the state's thoroughbred horses had to tell everything about a horse worth knowing.

Unfortunately, Governor Miller and his boastful aides had failed to consult with Northern New York's smugglers, bootleggers, and speakeasy operators on whether the war had been won against them. Despite the proud statements to the press and anyone else who would listen, North Country communities were still seeing heavily loaded vehicles filled with liquor and gun toting criminals whizzing through their downtowns.

TROOP B BLACK HORSE BRIGADE

CHAPTER 12

NEW YORK STATE POLICE WAGE WAR ON RUM RUNNERS

MALONE - For the 56 members of the New York State Police Black Horse Brigade who were assigned to the North Country along the international border, expectations were high that they could quickly stamp out the bootleggers, rumrunners and smugglers who were making a mockery of enforcement of the 18th Amendment to ban alcohol.[47]

Armed with a Winchester .30-30 rifle and a Colt .45, the troopers mounted on their black thoroughbred horses cut a dashing figure that captured the imagination of newspaper readers across the state.

New Yorkers who lived in metropolitan areas like New York City and the rural areas of upstate believed the assurances of the Albany politicians who claimed that these fearless young men, many of them veterans of World War 1, would be more than a match for the criminal element that continued to ignore the national prohibition against alcohol.

While the State Police had been established in 1917, the passage of Prohibition in 1920 provided them with their greatest test.

---

[47] History of the New York State Police, Website

The apparent failure of upstate New York's local, county, and federal law enforcement agencies to stamp out the problem prompted the same politicians who had promised that people would quickly quit drinking alcohol if Washington passed a law that expanding the state police would quickly end the daily reports that bootleggers were ignoring the law.

Headed by Captain C. J. Broadfield, the newly established statewide constabulary unit of 56 troopers in Malone had been chosen from among the best and brightest of young New Yorkers who saw the recently established law enforcement agency as an opportunity for a great adventure with an important mission - stamping out Demon Rum itself.

The reality of their day-to-day assignment may have seemed less than ideal as the newly sworn officers discovered their actual job was for pairs of troopers on horseback were expected to patrol 20-25 miles per day through the rural areas from small community to small community, often on dirt roads and trails, on extended patrols.

The New York State Police's founder and first Superintendent was George Fletcher Chandler who had been given the task of forming New York's first statewide police force even though he had no law enforcement experience. He was a doctor, not a lawman.

Born Dec. 13, 1872, in Clyde, N.Y., he graduated from Syracuse University in 1892 and went on to medical school at Columbia University College of Physicians and Surgeons, graduating in 1895.

He joined the New York National Guard, 10th NY Infantry Regiment as second lieutenant, and served as an assistant surgeon. By the time of the 1916 Mexican Incursion, he had risen to major, serving as adjutant of the 1st NY Provisional Brigade.

He had only recently returned from service along the Mexican border and was just beginning to establish his own medical practice when Gov. Charles Whitman appointed him the first Superintendent of the New York State Police on May 1, 1917.

Without previous police training or experience, Supt. Chandler assumed responsibility for everything from devising candidate selection methods and screening candidates, the Adirondack Enterprise wrote in an article exploring the history of the agency.

He conducted the physical examinations of his men personally. He supervised the development of his barracks in each region of the state. He designed the uniforms of the men who were soon known as the "Gray Riders" because of their dashing uniforms.

He bought them horses, developed procedures, and even chose the name by which members of the department would be forever known as New York State Troopers.

Superintendent Chandler's desire was to develop a professional, non-political police force. To accomplish this, he fought to maintain complete control over the department's hiring and firing practices. Many politicians tried to bully him into hiring their constituents, but Chandler steadfastly refused to accept any candidate who failed to meet his stringent requirements. Each man had to be "physically and mentally capable."

With no authorization to build barracks to house his men, Chandler devised a typically innovative plan: He would convince members of certain communities to build the barracks and rent them to the state. The plan worked so well that it later led to the construction of substations in many towns and villages. He also insisted on proper training for his men and established the first New York State School for Police. It was attended by local law enforcement officers as well as state troopers and was used as a model for several other states.

On Nov. 1, 1918, Supt. Chandler took leave from his duties with the state police to return to active military service. He served with the U.S. Army Medical Corps at Ft. Oglethorpe, Georgia from Nov.

1, 1918, to April 18, 1919. When he returned to Albany, he had to convince newly elected Gov. Alfred E. Smith that the New York State Police should be preserved. After a two-hour debate, the governor, a long-time NYSP opponent, reconsidered, saying, "I have changed my mind; now that we have a state police, let's make it the best there is."

Supt. Chandler remained with the New York State Police until Dec. 1, 1923, when he retired to resume his surgical practice. Under his skillful guidance, the New York State Police had been firmly established as a premier law enforcement agency.

Unfortunately, hamstrung by inadequate budgets and a fundamental misunderstanding of what it might take to plug the porous Northern New York border, the troopers soon discovered their beautiful thoroughbred horses were no match for the high powered touring cars and trucks that the smugglers could easily afford with the huge profits they could earn from a single run across the border.

Even worse, in many of the rural communities where they were expected to bring law and order, some of the residents found their puritanical mission to be an annoyance and a threat to those who saw Prohibition as more of an opportunity to pursue get rich quick schemes, than a holy crusade against immorality.

OGDENSBURG FAIRGROUNDS CROWD JEERS STATE TROOPERS

OGDENSBURG - When State Police from Troop B's barracks in Malone were assigned to help with crowd control at the car races at the Ogdensburg Fairgrounds (present athletic fields at Ogdensburg Free Academy), the troopers found themselves in a fist fight with some of the unruly audience members.[48]

---

[48] Malone Farmer, June 29, 1921

When a trooper ordered a spectator to get back, the crowd began jeering the officers.

During the ensuing shoving match, Trooper Conway was accused of striking James A. Bell in the face twice. Bell swore out a warrant for assault against the officer.

The Trooper filed a complaint charging Bell with disorderly conduct and resisting arrest.

When the cases came up in Justice Myron Gray's court, the Ogdensburg papers claimed the troopers, especially Sergeant Boyce, were disrespectful to the court, allegedly for trying to tell the judge his duties.

Ogdensburg Mayor Lynch wired Superintendent Chandler of the State Police that the city was "indignant."

He asked for an investigation and the recall of Sergeant Boyce.

Bell was acquitted by a jury. Charges were also dismissed against the state police sergeant.

Major Chandler provided no reply to Ogdensburg's Mayor.

TROOPERS CLASH WITH CHAMPLAIN POLICE CHIEF

CHAMPLAIN - The village of Champlain was the scene of a lively fracas Saturday night when the State Troopers came to a clash with the local officers of the law.[49]

As a result, the chief of police and one of the troopers took turns in occupying lockups, while the cause of all the trouble went free. According to the story, two State Troopers arrived in the village at about 9:30, and stationing themselves on the main street, began the enforcement of traffic regulations, relative to taillights and other vio-

---

[49] Chateaugay Record, Aug. 12, 1921

lations. A large crowd gathered to watch the operations, and it is said that several in the crowd began booing the troopers and shouting uncomplimentary remarks.

One young man who it appeared to the troopers was leading the booing ran into a barber shop when a trooper went to arrest him for disorderly conduct. A trooper followed him inside. Champlain Chief of Police Trombley was in the shop at the time. When the trooper demanded that the young man be turned over to him, the police chief responded that he, and he alone, would enforce the law in his community.

The trooper was then said to have demanded of the chief, his status in the village and to have pulled a gun.

Then it is alleged the chief seized the trooper by the neck - and backed him into a nearby corner. He afterwards took the trooper to the Champlain jail.

The other trooper in the meantime went for reinforcements and in a brief time arrived with a squad who went to the home of Chief Trombley and escorted him to the Rouses Point federal lockup.

Then they began the search for the original troublemaker, but he could not be found.

Chief Trombley was released on $200 bail and was told to appear for a hearing on the charge of assault. The president of the village made no statement regarding the affair other than that he expected to retain the chief.

The charges on both sides were eventually dismissed.

1920 CADILLAC
Oct. 21, 1921

CHAPTER **13**

TROOPER KILLS SMUGGLER DURING HIGH-SPEED CHASE, IN DEKALB, ST. LAWRENCE GRAND JURY INDICTS HIM

DEKALB - New York State Trooper Charles Spink hung on for dear life to the shiny new Cadillac as it pulled up behind the speeding roadster headed towards Gouverneur.[50]

Balancing himself precariously on the running board of the vehicle, the 23-year-old lawman could see in the glare of the headlights one of the fleeing bootleggers turn toward him and raise a gun.

Spink had already fired a round from his Colt .45 to convince the fleeing smugglers to pull over, but the criminals had ignored his warning shot.

As the two vehicles raced along the slippery, rain-soaked highway at over 50 miles per hour, the state trooper knew that he presented an inviting target to the gunman.

Eight months before, the Syracuse man had taken the oath, joining the newly organized New York State Police before being assigned to Potsdam in St. Lawrence County and Troop B.

---

[50] Ogdensburg Republican Journal, Oct. 13, 1921

152

During his training, he had been repeatedly warned by his instructors and superiors that this day might come.

Facing death, the trooper saw he had no choice but to fire his .45 caliber revolver at the gunman who had drawn a pistol on him.

He called to U.S. Customs Chief Henry Holland, who was inside the speeding vehicle, to ask whether he should fire at the smuggler who was aiming a gun at him.

He heard what he believed was the federal officer giving him permission to fire his weapon.

Despite the jostling of the high-powered Cadillac, he braced himself on his precarious perch as he balanced his body on the running board and aimed as best he could, remembering his training and pulling the trigger on his weapon, twice.

He felt the recoil and heard the sharp cracks of the heavy Colt .45.

Not long after Spink pulled the trigger, he saw the smuggler's car careen around a sharp turn as the bootleggers headed for Gouverneur.

The Cadillac that carried U.S. Customs officers and Trooper Spink attempted to follow the fleeing car around the curve, but skidded out of control, off the wet highway and into a pole.

Spink was thrown from his precarious position where he had been standing on the running board into a nearby field.

The man the trooper fired at was not so lucky.

Wilbur F. Hunt, a notorious Jefferson County smuggler, collapsed in his seat, dropping his pistol.

The trooper's bullet ended his life just moments before the Cadillac that carried Spinks and the Customs officers ran off the road, smashing into a pole.

As the New York State Police officer lay on the field with a broken leg, federal Customs officers got out of the wrecked Cadillac while the other law enforcement vehicle that had also been in pursuit of the rumrunners careened to a stop to come to their aid.

As the Customs officers helped Trooper Spink into the vehicle for the drive back to Ogdensburg to seek medical help, they promised themselves to do a better job of stopping the next smuggler who hauled a load of liquor through St. Lawrence County.

For Customs Chief Holland, the escape of the bootleggers was especially frustrating. Holland, a former Army Captain in Ogdensburg's Company M, had received information by telephone from one of his customs agents at the border near Fort Covington that the Chandler touring car, loaded with an illegal shipment of liquor, bar-

OCT. 12, 1921, EDITION OF OGDENSBURG'S REPUBLICAN JOURNAL

reled through the border checkpoint, making no attempt to report at the customs. Holland had immediately gathered Customs officers from Ogdensburg and asked for help from state police who had assigned Trooper Spinks from Potsdam and Trooper Deming from Hermon to help man the blockade they set up in Old DeKalb, where they awaited the liquor runners.

Letting them escape was a bitter pill for the Customs Director who oversaw federal operations across Northern New York.

But the next day, he discovered the bootlegger who had escaped the roadblock offered a wildly different version of the events as shown by this account reported in the Ogdensburg Republican Journal in the Oct. 12, 1921, edition. The headline shouted:

MURDER AND SHOOTING AT GOUVERNEUR ENDS RUNNING FIGHT IN AUTOS FROM OLD DEKALB
WATERTOWN BOOTLEGGER SHOT AND KILLED
COMPANION WOUNDED IN RUNNING FIGHT

All Roads in Northern New York Patrolled by Officers Seeking Assailants Who Escaped After Gunfire—Victim Is Wilbur Hunt Who Was Out on Bail for Volstead Violation—Simon Maynard of Philadelphia, N. Y. Driver of Car Detained by Police.

"Wilbur Hunt of 620 Addison Street, Watertown was shot and instantly killed and Simon Maynard of Philadelphia, N. Y. was shot in the arm, by unknown automobilists just outside the corporation limits of Gouverneur at midnight. [51]

"Every officer in northern New York is patrolling the highways looking for their assailants. The murder took place after a running

---

[51] Ogdensburg Republican Journal, Oct. 12, 1921

fight from Old DeKalb to Gouverneur, 14 miles. Hunt was shot in the chin, the bullet inflicting an ugly wound: Maynard, who is not seriously injured, says his companion died in his arms a few minutes after the shot was fired. The police believe the shooting was done by bootleggers

POLICE ARE NOTIFIED.

"Maynard, driving a high-powered Chandler touring car, drove into the village of Gouverneur at midnight with the dead man. The night officer there, Eugene Murphy, was notified and he immediately informed District Attorney William D. Ingram in this city (Ogdensburg) of the facts.

"Police officers at Watertown, Potsdam, Canton, and other surrounding towns were notified and within a brief time a network of officers was thrown around the northern roads. It is believed that the murderers cannot escape. A thorough search for them is being made. An inspection of the Chandler car revealed no liquor, but two loaded revolvers were found. There was nothing to indicate that shots had been fired from them. The Gouverneur police believe the shooting took place sometime before the report was made to them.

CHASED FOURTEEN MILES

"Maynard told the police he and his companion left Old DeKalb and that a short distance out of that town, he realized they were being pursued. The chase was kept up until the village of Gouverneur was sighted, he said. The shooting took place just after the car had passed two others on the road including a truck. The wound in the dead man's body would indicate that the pursuers were either ahead of them a short distance or that he was shot while looking backward. The wound indicates that the shot was fired from a rifle. Maynard, according to the police, was quite reticent and gave a hazy description of the occurrence. He said he was driving the car. Maynard, at the request of District Attorney Ingram, is being detained by the Gouverneur authorities. Hunt was about 40-years of age and Maynard is said to be around 80.

It was also reported last night that a car had been stolen at Malone but whether this had anything to do with the shooting remains to be developed. The murder aroused much excitement in Gouverneur and a crowd soon gathered in front of the police station awaiting the arrival of the coroner.

Mysterious Shooting

"Much mystery attaches itself to the shooting. Maynard, police say, has given no plausible explanation for his car being chased such a considerable distance. He claims no shots were fired until Gouverneur was in sight. It was also reported that two cars pursued the Maynard car, both filled with men. The police were quickly placed along the state highways and town roads. Woods were being searched and a close inspection made of farmyards and meadows. Every available officer within a radius of several miles was notified of the murder and were given strict orders to keep a thorough watch of the highways.

Hunt Out on Bail

"At Watertown last night it was stated by Chief of Police Edward J. Singleton that Hunt was a carpenter in that city and was under indictment and out on bail for a violation of the Volstead law, growing out of the Beckstead case which it is said, involved the theft of some whiskey from a resident of Carthage. Hunt, it is said, at the time of his arrest on this charge denied going to Carthage with Beckstead, who was shot in the escape, but stated that at the request of a man named Bass, he brought the load of liquor to Binghamton - where he sold it- procuring $2,250, part of which he admitted turning over to Bass.

"The theory among some officers is that the shooting last night was an aftermath of this case and that it was a "bootleggers feud with a desire of evening up, although Chief Singleton said that while he had only a partial knowledge of the facts, that he did not share this view.

INVESTIGATION TODAY.

"District Attorney Ingram will conduct a full investigation of the case today.

For the federal Customs officers and New York State troopers involved in the high-speed chase and shooting, discovering that one of the bootleggers they had been chasing died and that the other smuggler was now claiming that they were somehow the victims came as a major shock.

Especially after they read what some of the newspapers were reporting based on the claims of the bootleggers who had evaded capture.

It did not take the federal and state officers long for them to offer their own, decidedly quite different version of the events that had led up to Wilbur Hunt's shooting.

The Ogdensburg Republican Journal's headline reported in the Oct. 13, 1921, edition:

FATAL SHOT FIRED BY TROOPER SPINK, WAS ACCOMPANYING PARTY OF FEDERAL OFFICERS

Bootleggers Failed to Halt When Ordered and as One of Them Was Preparing to Return Fire of Pursuers, State Trooper Charles Spink Shot Twice, One of Bullets Grazing Driver's Arm and Second Killing Hunt, His Companion,

Technical Charge of Manslaughter Lodged Against Spink—Collector Henry Holland Headed Party of Pursuing Officers—District Attorney Ingram Gives Out Results of Investigation—Spink's Hearing Set for This Afternoon

As a result of an investigation conducted by District Attorney William D. Ingram, assisted by St. Lawrence County Sheriff Lawrence Fishback at Gouverneur and Canton into the circumstances surrounding the shooting of Wilbur Hunt of Watertown early yesterday morning on the state road near Gouverneur, it was established that the fatal shot was fired by State Trooper Charles Spink while accompanying a party of United States Customs officers headed by Collector Henry Holland of Ogdensburg who were pursuing the liquor laden car occupied by Hunt and Lynn Maynard of Philadelphia, N.Y. [52]

Trooper Spink was placed under arrest on a technical charge of manslaughter and was charged with a crime before Justice of the Peace Leon C. Crary at Canton. The case was adjourned until today at 2 p.m. at Ogdensburg. It was brought out that Collector Holland had received word on Tuesday that a liquor car was expected to pass along the road toward Gouverneur during the night. He summoned a party of federal officers and State Troopers Spink and Demming of Hermon and started for the scene. They posted themselves along the road and waited. When the car which they sought made its appearance, the order was given to halt, but the driver continued. One or two shots were fired by the officers and the chase began. As the two cars approached the village of Richville, Trooper Spink, who was standing on the running board of the pursuing car, is alleged to have fired two more shots, one of which grazed the arm of Maynard while

---

[52] Ogdensburg Republican Journal, Oct. 13, 1921

the other struck Hunt on the point of his chin, passing down into his neck and causing instant death. As Maynard kept on and the pursuing car was compelled to abandon the chase because of crashing into a telegraph pole, the pursuing party were unaware that either of the shots had taken effect and did not ascertain this fact until yesterday morning. Sheriff Fishback, who was out all night on the case after being called to Gouverneur, learned from Coroner Allen at Richville that it was reported that State Troopers had fired upon an automobile near there the previous night. The sheriff upon returning to Canton looked up Trooper Spink and asked him about the report. Up to that time Spink did not know that anyone had been shot the previous night. He told the sheriff about the occurrence and accompanied him back to Gouverneur to relate his story to the District Attorney. About 2 o'clock yesterday morning Police Officers Nicholson, Farley, and McCormick, who at the direction of District Attorney Ingram were watching the Canton Road for incoming cars, halted two machines at the junction of the state highway and the Arnold Road, about two miles out of the city. The first car contained Collector Holland and William H. Pearson and the second was a closed Cadillac, with the front and top damaged, driven by a federal government employee from Rouses Point. The police officers asked the motorists if they had heard about a man being shot near Gouverneur and they said no. Capt. Holland explained that the rear car had met with an accident. The party then went ahead.

Later, after his arrival in the village of Gouverneur, District Attorney Ingram assembled the various threads of the story, and the results of his investigations are in the following statement which he made last night to the press upon his return home.

"The facts are as follows: Capt. Holland received word from reliable sources that a load of whiskey was preparing to pass Old Dekalb toward Gouverneur. He got the officers together and sent two State

Troopers. Trooper Charles Spink of Potsdam and Trooper Demming of Hermon came to Ogdensburg and conferred with Capt. Holland Tuesday night. The cars with the officers then started for Old Dekalb; and stationed themselves along the highway between Old Dekalb and Richville. About midnight, a car came running in the direction of Richville from Old Dekalb and the customs officers and troopers at that time were stationed along the highway. The car was ordered to halt but the driver increased his speed. One or two shots were fired by the officers, but the car continued on its way. The car containing Capt. Holland and two or three revenue officers, and the troopers started in pursuit of the other car. The car ahead traveled at a very rapid rate of speed and it was difficult to keep up with it. Trooper Charles Spink was standing on the right-hand running board of the car containing the revenue officers. As the cars approached Richville, and just before they entered the village, Spink fired two more shots. One of these shots struck the handle of the wheel of the auto and grazed the left forearm of the driver, Lynn Maynard, of the town of Philadelphia.

Maynard says that as he was driving along, Hunt said, "They are shooting, and Maynard said he replied, "I'd shoot back."

With that Hunt reached for a gun and turned, halfway in his seat preparatory to shooting back at the pursuers. It was just as he turned around in his seat and looked back that he received the wound that caused his death.

The shot struck Wilbur Hunt of Watertown in the chin. With that, Hunt fell over backward against the windshield and said, "Oh, I'm gone."

"In that connection, Trooper Spink, before I interviewed Maynard, stated that he saw this man turn in his seat and he thought he saw something in his hand and that this is when he shot.

"The cars continued. The driver of the first car, Maynard, made the last turn toward Gouverneur safely but the pursuing car went straight ahead and hit a telegraph pole, breaking it in two and damaging the car: At this the chase was abandoned. Maynard drove ahead toward Gouverneur (and after making the turn, pushed the dead man into the corner of the car. He then drove to the next turn in Gouverneur, which is a left-hand turn and about one-half mile from where the chase was abandoned. He then drove to the left again and took the country road for two miles to the farm of George Pike.

"When he got there, he deposited his load of liquor in the back of the buildings on the farm, pulled the dead man over into the back of the car and proceeded to Gouverneur and to the office of Dr. Webster.

Dr. Webster examined him and stated that he must have been instantly killed. Dr. Webster then called up Night Chief Eugene Murphy at police headquarters and Murphy then called me.

"The car contained eight cases of rye whiskey, a quantity of Scotch whiskey, some gin and a case of wine. It was going to Watertown. The pursuing car contained, besides the driver, Capt. Holland, William H. Pearson, Trooper Dimming and Trooper Spink, who was on the running board.

"Today I went to Gouverneur, and Trooper Spink made a complete statement to me of the whole transaction., I also interviewed Maynard and found that he was represented by (former St. Lawrence County District Attorney and D.A. Ingram's former long-time boss) James C. Dolan of Gouverneur. Mr. Maynard made a complete statement in the presence of Mr. Dolan, Sheriff Fishbeck, and me. In that statement he told us of having entered the bootlegging business this summer and how he had made several trips to Fort Covington and the border for liquor. He stated that he and Hunt left home Tuesday about noon, went to Fort Covington, crossed the border two or three miles to a farmhouse where they had supper, obtained the liquor, and started back home. Hunt was driving the car. They got astray before they got to Potsdam, but they finally made their way through to Potsdam. At that point, Hunt asked Maynard to drive, stating to him that they were past the danger. Maynard took the wheel and was driving at the time of the shooting. He says he saw the cars lined up on the road near Old Dekalb but that he heard no command to halt and when they started to fire, he thought they were robbers, and he sped up to get away. He nearly tipped over two or three times because of the speed he was traveling but in making the turns he kept to the inside of the curb, hugging the turns.

I asked him if he had any idea who shot Hunt and he said 'No, unless it was Beckstead or some of that gang,' but he said he had no way of knowing whether it was them or not.

"Maynard had told in his statement previously that he had agreed to sell 'to a man he took for Hunt a load of booze and that 'he went to the border,' got the liquor and returned to what is known as the Northshore of Guffin's Bay and there - delivered over the liquor to a man he thought to be Hunt but who turned out to be another man. He claimed he never received pay for his load, and he named men who were in the deal and others with whom he had dealings.

(The District Attorney stated that this part of the affair related to prior transactions.)

"As a result of the investigation it was deemed advisable to prefer a charge of manslaughter against Trooper Charles Spink," which was accordingly done before Justice of the Peace Leon C. Crary at Canton. The officer was arraigned, and the case adjourned until Thursday at 2 p.m., and it was transferred to Ogdensburg for a hearing." District Attorney Ingram stated that another arrest might be made today. He said that the officials of the State Troopers would be called here and requested to show if the troopers had any right to cooperate with the federal officers. Mr. Ingram added that he knew the troopers had done so in the past. Collector Holland was present at the hearing in Canton. U.S. President Woodrow Wilson appointed Holland to be the Collector of Customs in Ogdensburg. The appointment overseeing the Port of Ogdensburg, and the U.S. Customs crossings in Northern New York was considered one of the better paying political appointments available for loyal party supporters like Holland who had agreed to run as the Democratic congressional candidate in the 26th District in both 1902 and 1904.

The Collector of Customs in Ogdensburg was paid $5,000 a year ($80,000 a year in today's dollars), plus a percentage of the fees collected from tariffs and duties collected at Northern New York's ports. Ogdensburg's salary was equal to Los Angeles, California, Norfolk Va., and Galveston Texas.

On October 14th, Ogdensburg's Republican Journal reported the jarring news that U.S. Customs Collector Henry Holland, Ogdensburg's top federal Customs officer overseeing border crossings stretching from Oswego to Rouses Point had been arrested:

US CUSTOMS COLLECTOR HOLLAND ARRESTED, MATTER IS SENT TO JANUARY TERM OF THE GRAND JURY; DISTRICT ATTORNEY MAKES CHARGE OF MANSLAUGHTER IN FIRST DEGREE AGAINST FEDERAL OFFICIAL SAME AS PREFERRED AGAINST STATE TROOPER SPINKS WHO FIRED FATAL SHOT - LATTER'S HEARING SET DOWN FOR OCT. 22, COUNSEL FOR COLLECTOR ISSUES STATEMENT ON SHOOTING SAYING CLIENT VOLUNTARILY SUBMITS TO JURISDICTION OF COURT AND DESIRES INVESTIGATION BY GRAND JURY

He was accompanied by Attorney George E. Van Kennen. Maynard was charged with a crime before Justice Arthur Abbott at Gouverneur and waived examination. [53]

---

[53] Ogdensburg Republican Journal, Oct. 14, 1921

He was held for the grand jury on $1,000 bail on a charge of illegally transporting liquor. The autopsy on the body of Hunt was performed by Coroner F. D. Allen of Richville, assisted by Dr. Youngs of Gouverneur. The coroner's report had not been received by District Attorney Ingram last night. The bullet which killed Hunt was fired from an automatic pistol of .45 caliber The dead man had an automatic pistol on his person and the driver of the car was similarly armed. Maynard told the District Attorney that he had a gun license which was issued to him by Judge Conboy of Jefferson County, When District Attorney Ingram arrived at Gouverneur he found Chief of Police Singleton of Watertown and Sheriff Gillette of Jefferson County awaiting him, but as soon as they discovered that it was a matter for the St. Lawrence County officials, they withdrew. Four federal prohibition agents also made their appearance and wanted to take charge of the liquor, but District Attorney Ingram refused to permit them to interfere with it, as it was in the custody of the officials of St. Lawrence County. The prohibition agents contented themselves with attaching identification notices on the packages. The liquor and the car, a seven-passenger Chandler, also seized by the county officials, will be removed to Canton today. Meanwhile they are in the custody of the chief of police of Gouverneur, who was notified by the District Attorney to permit no one to touch them.

NEW YORK STATE POLICE LIEUTENANT DEFENDS TROOPER

When New York State Police Lieutenant Walter Crosdale arrived in Canton after the shooting, he wasted no time issuing a strongly worded statement defending the actions of his trooper in the shooting death of the armed bootlegger and smuggler.[54]

---

[54] Ogdensburg Republican Journal, Oct. 14, 1921

"The shooting of Wilbur F. Hunt of Watertown by Trooper Charles Spink last Tuesday night in the running gun battle near Gouverneur was a regrettable accident which cannot be cleared up until the varying statements of the principals can be threshed out in court. It must be remembered, however, that Spink is sworn to uphold the laws and constitution of the United States and this state, that he stood on the running board of an automobile, a plain target for Hunt, a desperado, whiskey smuggler and gunman, who was aiming to snuff out the trooper's life.

Lieut. Croasdale discussed the shooting at length, telling the North Country's press of the narrow escapes from death the troopers face daily at the hands of whiskey runners, a large majority of whom are not natives of the North Country, but who are professional gunmen of New York, Utica, and other cities, many with long criminal records.

Trooper Spink, since being paroled in my custody, has been at the barracks (in Malone)," he said. "He is still limping and suffering from injuries that he sustained when the car in which he was riding struck a pole. Spink is a straight, clean-cut youngster of about 23 years, six feet one inch in height, and of splendid physique. His home is in Syracuse, and he has been in the service for the past eight months. He has a splendid record, not a mark against him.

Of course, there is a variance in the statements of Spink and Port Collector Henry Holland of Ogdensburg. Spink says Holland told him to fire; Holland denies the assertion. Which is true, I do not know. That is a matter that will have to be threshed out before the grand jury or in court. The situation is that Holland had information that Hunt and Lynn Maynard of Philadelphia were coming through with a load of liquor. He called in some of his men to assist in the capture and asked for help from us. Trooper Spink was detailed and therefore came under the direction of Holland, for when working with federal officers our men naturally obey their orders. The smugglers had been commanded to halt; that they did not hear may be true, that we do not know. At any rate, the chase was on, and it was evident to Hunt and Maynard, according to the latter's own statement, that they were being pursued. To force the fleeing car to halt, Spink fired. He was standing out on the running board of the big limousine, which was racing over the slippery, rain-soaked highway at a suicidal rate of 50 miles an hour. The cars were but a few feet apart, the lights of the car carrying the officers shining on the speeding machine ahead.

Spink says he saw Hunt turn and raise his revolver. The trooper in his position on the running board was a plain target for the law-breaker, who was determined upon escape with his valuable load of contraband. Self-preservation is the first law of nature; troopers are armed by the state to protect themselves in encounters with the law-less element. Spink fired and the bullet caused Hunt's death. Accurate aim at the rate the cars were rushing along was impossible, that the bullet took effect as it did was a matter of chance.

The average citizen is not aware of the problems and difficulties that confront the troopers and Customs men along this northern border in preventing the smuggling of intoxicants and other goods, too. We are up here in a wild country where even many of the people have no feeling of friendship for us. It is not the natives of Northern New York, however, who give us the most trouble, it is the desperate gunmen who in a tight situation do not hesitate to fire upon an officer, who make the work of troopers dangerous.

These gunmen of the Hunt and Maynard type come through here from Watertown, Utica, New York, and other cities. They drive north in high powered automobiles. Passing over the line, they buy whiskey at from $40 to $60 a case. Sometimes they must spend several days getting a load. In New York they get around $100 for it. After a load is secured and the dash for the market starts, it takes more than kind words to bring them within the arm of the law. You cannot go out on the highway, when these desperadoes come racing along, and say, 'Please, mister, will you let me see if you are smuggling whiskey?' Such methods would produce nothing more than trooper funerals, for the smugglers shoot quickly and to kill.

It was only a few nights ago that I was driving into Malone at about 3 in the morning. It was a rainy, disagreeable night and I was hurrying to get into headquarters. Along the road I passed a car but paid no heed to it. A second after I had passed the machine, fire opened on me. Another instance revealing the abandon with which these criminals handle firearms is illustrated in the case of a customs officer near Rouses Point a brief time ago. Driving an automobile along the road and not noticing anyone, he was fired upon, and shots riddled the back of his car.

There is no doubt that we are fighting the worst element of gun-fighters from the cities, for on two occasions we have captured some of them. There was the case a few weeks ago of a gang of Utica gun-men who held off Customs officers at gunpoint before we captured them.

On another occasion we got several New York gangsters, all tot-ing guns, and black jacks.

Asked about the report of Gouverneur physicians who com-plained that their cars were halted along the road the same night and that some of them were roughly handled, Lieut. Croasdale said he had not before heard of the incident.

Walter Hunt may have been a stranger in St. Lawrence County, but the press soon discovered that he was well known as a gunman and booze runner in Jefferson County.

He was also known as someone who was not afraid to double cross his own associates to make a few extra bucks in the illegal smug-gling and bootlegging business, even if it cost someone their life.

Just weeks before his death, Hunt had been arrested in Jefferson County for helping members of a Jefferson County-based criminal gang who murdered a rival and hijacked a booze shipment.

An article offered a picture of who this bootlegger was who had died in the high-speed gun battle on the rural backroads of DeKalb in St. Lawrence County and the kind of men he associated with in Watertown.

SMUGGLER HUNT NO STRANGER TO BOOTLEGGING, ASSOCIATES INDICTED IN SENSATIONAL MURDER

WATERTOWN, Oct. 12. —Hunt is no stranger to the bootlegging business. Hunt was arrested on Sept. 12 by the Watertown police at his residence, charged with the transportation of 212 cases of whiskey and gin through this city on July 29, in the company of Merton P. Bass.[55]

Hunt was also charged in connection with the possession of 35 bottles of mixed brands of whiskey, gin, and vermouth at his residence on Sept. 12 when the officers placed him under arrest. The police confiscated the alcohol but there was no warrant issued for his arrest on the possession charge, it being decided to present the facts to the grand jury to be used in considering the transportation allegation. Attorney H. C. Teepell represented Hunt.

Bass was recently arrested in connection with a sensational liquor robbery in Carthage that left Loren Beckstead shot in the chest in Carthage in July.

Merton P. Bass of Watertown, George A. Humphrey of Cape Vincent have all been charged for their roles in the robbery of fellow

---

[55] Ogdensburg Republican Journal, Oct. 13, 1921

bootlegger James C. Marsh of Carthage that ended in the shooting of Loren Beckstead, one of the team of hijackers.

The authorities allege that Beckstead, Bass and Humphrey stole the liquor from Marsh at Carthage on the morning of July 29.

After Beckstead was shot during the robbery, Bass drove his mortally wounded fellow hijacker back towards Watertown, but instead of seeking medical help, he stopped to hide the stolen whiskey and gin in a clump of bushes on the old state street highway to Carthage.

He then brought Beckstead to his State Street residence, instead of the hospital or to a doctor.

Immediately after leaving Beckstead at home to fend for himself, Bass went to Hunt's residence. Beckstead eventually died from his injuries.

While Beckstead lay dying at his residence, Bass and Hunt went to where the liquor was hidden, loaded the booze in their vehicle and drove to the Lake Ontario community of Chaumont where it was kept until the following day.

On July 30, Hunt and Bass were charged with going to Binghamton from Chaumont, driving through the city with the 22 cases of "wet goods," where it was sold.

Hunt insisted to police, following his arrest, he was not in any way involved in the theft of the liquor from Marsh.

Hunt testified that Bass and himself sold 21 cases of liquor and the money was divided between the two.

Although Bass returned to Watertown immediately after the transaction, Hunt remained for the next several weeks at Rochester. He arrived in Watertown about Sept. 11 and the next day he was arrested.

Beckstead, Bass and Humphrey are facing a first-degree robbery charge.

Hunt denied emphatically to the police that he had a role in the murder of Beckstead, although he admitted he split the proceeds of the robbery with Bass.

Marsh is charged with a liquor violation for alleged possession.

For many years Hunt was employed "as a carpenter with Gorman B. Hayes; contractor of this city." Hunt and his wife, Ina, have two sons, Frederick, an independent contractor and Wilbur, Jr., who works for a concrete company. He also has an eight-year-old daughter, Gladys. Hunt is survived by his wife.

Maynard is a farmer who breeds Ayrshire cattle.

On Oct. 13, 1921, U.S. Customs Chief for the Northern District of New York, Henry Holland, was arrested for his role in the shooting death of the notorious bootlegger.

The Ogdensburg Journal Headline read:

DISTRICT ATTORNEY INGRAM MAKES CHARGE OF MANSLAUGHTER IN FIRST DEGREE AGAINST FEDERAL OFFICIAL, SAME AS WAS PREFERRED AGAINST STATE TROOPER SPINKS, WHO FIRED FATAL SHOT—LATTER'S HEARING SET DOWN FOR OCT. 22—COUNSEL FOR COLLECTOR ISSUES STATEMENT ON SHOOTING, SAYING CLIENT VOLUNTARILY SUBMITS TO JURISDICTION OF COURT AND DESIRES INVESTIGATION BY ST. LAWRENCE COUNTY GRAND JURY

OGDENSBURG - Yesterday's developments in the Wilbur Hunt shooting case were the arraignment of State Trooper Charles H. Spinks, who fired the fatal shot, before Justice of the Peace Myron E. Gray of this city, the adjournment of the hearing to October 22nd at 1:30 p.m. and the formal arrest and arraignment of United States Collector of Customs Henry Holland for manslaughter in the first degree, the same as was

> made against Trooper Spinks before Justice of the Peace Leon Crary at Canton Wednesday.[56]

Captain Holland, through his attorney, George E. Van Kennen, waived examination, and the case was sent to the January term of the St. Lawrence grand jury for investigation.

Bail was fixed at $1,000 by St. Lawrence County Judge John C. Crapser who was in the city and who went with Captain Holland and his counsel to the courtroom at the request of Mr. Van Kennen for this purpose, Justice Gray not having the authority to fix the bond. Former Ogdensburg Mayor Julius Frank and S. W. Leroux put up the bond guaranteeing the Custom's Chief's appearance to face charges.

St. Lawrence County District Attorney William D. Ingram stood for the people in both cases.

The complaint in the case of Captain Holland was made by the District Attorney and the warrant was issued in the courtroom by Justice Gray. Ogdensburg Police Chief John D. McCormick was called from police headquarters to serve the warrant upon Collector Holland.

The entire proceeding lasted but a few moments. District Attorney Ingram had indicated Wednesday night upon his return from Gouverneur and Canton, where he spent the day investigating the case, that he would lodge a formal charge against the Customs chief yesterday, in view of the fact that he was in charge of the party of federal officers and State Troopers who were pursuing the liquor car when the shooting of Hunt occurred.

Captain Holland was notified to this effect by the District Attor-

[56] Ogdensburg Republican Journal, Oct. 14, 1921

ney, and he held himself in readiness to appear with his counsel when the case was called shortly before 3 p.m.

Attorney Van Kennen stated to the court at the beginning of the proceeding that his client was averse to being arrested but that he submitted voluntarily to the authority of the court and considered it proper that an investigation into the matter be conducted by the St. Lawrence County grand jury.

He said the Customs Collector had been reliably informed that a liquor car was to pass over the road Tuesday night and that in the discharge of his duty, he had summoned the officers and set out to intercept the violators of the law after having been criticized. What happened after that, he added, was a matter of common knowledge.

"We appear voluntarily and ask for an investigation," declared the attorney. During his remarks Mr. Van Kennen also referred to the statement given to the papers by District Attorney Ingram, declaring it was exceedingly rare, barring one or two incidents, which he did not specify.

District Attorney Ingram said it would be necessary to follow the usual procedure of serving the warrant and making the arraignment before the case was sent to the grand jury.

After these formalities had been complied with, counsel for the defendant stated that the Customs collector would waive examination and furnish bail in any sum required by the court.

Ogdensburg's Advance and St. Lawrence Weekly Democrat George Darrow, one of the North Country's leading advocates for Prohibition, wasted little time coming to the defense of the state trooper and Customs Director Holland, a fellow Democrat.

In his Oct. 20th edition, Darrow argued in his headline:

OFFICERS WERE DOING THEIR DUTY, DRIVER REFUSED TO STOP.

He also stressed that Wilbur F. Hunt of Watertown was an indicted bootlegger who refused to obey the lawful orders of both the state police and U.S. Customs officers.[57]

"The arrest of Capt. Holland caused considerable talk in the city and sides have been taken, those who believe in the liquor traffic being against Holland, while those who believe in the law's enforcement are standing solidly behind him. The greatest criticism which is leveled against Holland is that he should not personally have headed the manhunt for the smugglers but should have sent out his deputies. The majority gives him credit for not shirking his duty and for being willing to take the same chances faced by any of his deputies. He was doing his duty and was trying to run down men who were evading the customs officials. He expresses regret over the shooting and none of the officers knew that anyone had been hit as the automobile which they were chasing continued its way, going at a terrific clip. The first knowledge that the state troopers and Capt. Holland had thought that a man had been killed when they heard of it the next morning. Trooper Spink told Sheriff Fishbeck that it must be the men they were after the night before.

At Old Dekalb, Collector Holland and his men made a stand. One car was placed across the road, but it had to be removed to allow another automobile to pass. Before it could be replaced, the car containing the whiskey smugglers came along at a speed estimated at fifty miles an hour. They were ordered to halt but refused to do so. The authorities then started after them, both cars going at a terrific pace, with Spink standing on the running board of one of the limousines. The chase continued through Richville and on to Gouverneur, as they reached the Dony Coarse farm, one of the occupants of the smugglers' car was seen rising in his seat with a gun in his hand.

---

[57] Ogdensburg Advance and Weekly St. Lawrence Democrat, Oct. 20, 1921

When Spink saw his life was in danger, he fired from the moving vehicle, not aware he had killed the gunman until the next day.

About the time of the shooting, the driver of the car in which the trooper was riding lost control, due to the excessive speed and crashed into a telephone pole, breaking it in half, injuring the trooper as well as the car. The smugglers were then able to escape, and the chase was discontinued without the Customs men knowing the result of the chase.

According to the story told by Maynard, one of the shots killed Hunt instantly and the other took effect in his arm. He managed to keep the wheel, however, and swung the car off onto the Scotch Settlement Road at the junction of the River Road into Gouverneur.

There, he hid his liquor, after which he drove to the farm of George Pike, the well-known Ayrshire breeder, and asked him to telephone for a doctor.

Upon the arrival of the physician, he announced that Hunt was dead and died instantly. The authorities were immediately notified, and the car was taken to Gouverneur where Maynard was charged before Justice Arthur Abbott and held with $1,000 bail for transporting liquor.

Hides Booze with Dead Companion in Seat.

Save the alcohol was the one thought of Maynard. He did not know whether his companion was dead or alive as he lay crumpled up on the seat of the car and seemed to care more if the liquor could be saved.

Instead of driving to Gouverneur for medical aid, he spends considerable time hiding his load. Against the load of alcohol, a human life means nothing to him. The autopsy found that Hunt had been killed by a 45-caliber revolver. Maynard had a license to carry a gun, the same having been issued to him by County Judge Conboy of Jefferson County on Sept. 6th.

The whiskey which Maynard had caught was found on the Pike farm behind an old shed. In a statement which Maynard made to District Attorney William D. Ingram he said that he entered the smuggling business last summer and had made several trips to Fort Covington and the border for liquor.

He and Hunt, he said, left home Tuesday and crossed the border at Fort Covington, going about three miles into Canada where they obtained the liquor and then started for home.

Hunt had a record as a bootlegger and was known as a reckless driver and dangerous gunman by the Customs authorities. He was under indictment and out on bail for his connection with the Carthage bootlegging case last summer in which a man named Beckstead was shot. Several bottles of liquor were found in the car after Hunt's body was removed. Maynard is a native of Dexter, where he was born 20 years ago, the son of Mr. and Mrs. Julius Maynard. The family lived for several years on a farm in the Luther Hill settlement. About four years ago the farm was sold, the family moved to the village and are living on what is known as the old Snooks farm on Pillar Point Road. Maynard conducted a milk route until his removal to Philadelphia about two years ago. He was married to Dexter about eight years ago. When he went to Philadelphia his father went with him, the mother being dead. Maynard bought the old Holmes farm of Henry and Frank Hagan located off the Antwerp Road about three miles from the village, paying about $18,000 for it.

He was considered a prosperous farmer and a hard worker and his reputation both in Dexter and Philadelphia has always been the best. He bore the respect of all who knew him and the escapade in which he figured came as a complete surprise and shock to his friends. He has no children. According to a report in Philadelphia,

Hunt is alleged to have come to Maynard and offered him $10 to make the trip with him to Canada. Maynard is said to have invested no money in the liquor, although it is said that upon reaching Canada, Hunt borrowed $120 of him with which to pay for the load.

Attorney Van Kennen's Statement.

Because the injury to Wilber F. Hunt occurred while the Customs officers, assisted by the state troopers, were in the discharge of their duty to apprehend Hunt and his companion, Lynn Maynard. while violating the customs law as well as the Mullan-Gage law. Collector of Customs Henry Holland today decided to appear before a magistrate in this city and voluntarily submit to its authority in order that the facts may be investigated by the grand jury.

District Attorney Ingram was present. The collector waived examination and gave bail in the sum of $1,000 to await the action of the grand jury. It was decided this was the best course to pursue under the circumstances in order that all facts might be brought out with relation to the unfortunate accident that happened near Dekalb in this county. Technically, the members of the party were under the direction of the Collector and were trying to apprehend Hunt and Maynard in the act of transporting contraband liquors smuggled from Canada. Subsequent events show that the information which the collector received to the effect that an attempt would be made on that night to run an automobile load of liquors through the county was true. The Customs officers made no mistake in challenging the Hunt car when it attempted to pass with its load of liquors. The driver of the auto refused to stop his car when ordered to do so, and instead put on speed, taking a chance of making the run to safety. Everyone regrets the unfortunate accident that befell Hunt. Nevertheless, the Customs officers as well as the troopers appear to have been well within their rights in attempting to prevent open and flagrant violation of the law. The unfortunate accident would have been prevented had the occupants of the automobile obeyed the signal to stop for Customs purposes. The state troopers were present for the purpose of assisting the Customs officers in the prevention of crime and the arrest of the criminals.

PHYSICIANS COMPLAIN OVER TREATMENT AT DEKALB ROADBLOCK

An Oct. 15, 1921, edition of the Ogdensburg Republican Journal reported that a group of physicians had been traveling through Old DeKalb the night of the shooting.[58]

Dr. Sayer, one of the Gouverneur physicians who were held up by the party of officers patrolling the road near Old DeKalb, called up District Attorney Ingram and gave his version of the affair.

He said they left Ogdensburg at 11:40 p.m. and when nearing Old DeKalb, heard shooting.

They were halted by a group of men who asked whether they had any liquor. The men ordered the doctors to get out of the car as they wanted to search it. They ordered the driver to stop his engine. One of the searchers felt Dr. Sayer's pockets and thought he had discovered a weapon, but it proved to be the physician's stethoscope.

Dr. Sayer said to the District Attorney: "These men acted like brigands. If they were officers, they did not show their authority, and we thought they were highwaymen. I thought I saw one man in uniform in the crowd."

Mr. Ingram stated that federal agents attempted to confiscate the liquor that had been seized as part of the investigation. He refused, saying that if the evidence was allowed to be taken away from the county authorities, he would find it necessary to let Maynard go, as he would have nothing to hold him on. He said the federal prohibi-

---

[58] Ogdensburg Republican Journal, Oct. 15, 1921

tion agents had nothing whatever to do with the arrest of Maynard or the seizure of the liquor and car and that they did not make their appearance in Gouverneur until several hours later.

Meanwhile, the District Attorney had directed that the property be held in the custody of the Gouverneur chief until it was delivered to the sheriff and this arrangement was approved by James C. Dolan, defense counsel for Maynard. When the prohibition agents sought to take the property away, they were told that they could not do so, and they proceeded to attach seals to the car and the liquor. Later, it was found that the notice attached to the radiator pipe by the Gouverneur Police Chief had been torn off and thrown on the floor and this was replaced.

District Attorney Ingram spoke plainly in expressing his disgust over the unprofessional conduct of the four federal agents as well as the conduct of other federal prohibition agents who have worked in this county.

He recalled that one had gotten into trouble for padding his expense accounts, that one McPhillips failed to keep his promise to appear to answer a charge made against him in the county courts and that a third had been publicly intoxicated in the streets of Potsdam.

Mr. Ingram stated that because of the conduct of these prohibition agents he had some time ago sent a formal protest about their continued presence to federal enforcement headquarters. District Attorney Ingram said he would fight to "the last ditch any attempt on the part of the federal agents to remove the evidence in the Maynard case from the custody of the county authorities as an unwarrantable interference and if they persisted he would go to the St. Lawrence County Grand Jury and ask that they be indicted under federal law for interfering in his investigation.

INDIGNATION EXPRESSED IN WATERTOWN OVER SHOOTING

WATERTOWN, Oct. 14. —General indignation is being expressed here at the methods used by officials in the shooting of Wilbur J. Hunt of this city near Richville Wednesday morning and the unlawful holdup of Gouverneur physicians near Old DeKalb. [59]

Similar methods were severely criticized by leading lawyers of the Jefferson County bar last spring when George W. Reeves, former county judge of Jefferson County, characterized conditions as a "reign of terror." Shooting at motorists without search warrants or other legal reasons last spring brought about the operations of robbers who imitated the officers, and it is feared that similar acts will follow the present methods.

(Leading Watertown lawyers yesterday asserted that officers, without a warrant, have no right to hold up a motorist proceeding along the highway, nor to open fire on him.

"There is no legal difference between a man in uniform, armed with a government gun, and a citizen, unless the officer has a "warrant," said John B. Rogers.

"It might have been you or me," remarked Judge George W. Beeves in discussing the shooting of Hunt.

"What right does any man have to tell a person on the highway? Absolutely none unless he has a warrant," was the opinion of Henry J. Kimball.

---

[59] Ogdensburg Republican Journal, Oct. 15, 1921

FEDERAL MAGISTRATE OBJECTS TO MAYNARD'S RELEASE

WATERTOWN, Oct. 14. - A federal magistrate is objecting to St. Lawrence County court officials' decision to release one of the gunmen involved in the high-speed gunfight in Dekalb that resulted in the death of a notorious Watertown bootlegger and smuggler.

Lynn Maynard of Philadelphia who was with Wilber F. Hunt when he was shot near Gouverneur Tuesday night, and who has been released on $1,000 bail after being arraigned on a charge of transportation, and possession of' intoxicants in violation of a state law, may be rearrested and called upon to face a federal warrant charging importation, transportation and smuggling of liquors.

GRAND JURY CHOOSES NOT TO INDICT OFFICERS, BUT ASKS FOR TROOPER'S DISMISSAL FOR KILLING SMUGGLER

Two months later, the manslaughter case took a dramatic turn when the St. Lawrence County Grand Jury chose not to indict either officer but did issue a critical report of the actions of Customs Collector Henry Holland and the state police officer who fired the fateful shot, recommending that Trooper Charles Spinks be fired.

The Ogdensburg Advance and St. Lawrence Weekly Democrat reported on Jan. 26, 1922, that criminals across the North Country were celebrating the Grand Jury's decision, suggesting that St. Lawrence County authorities had sent a clear message that law enforcement could expect little in the way of support in their fight against the gangsters who were hauling loads of illegal liquor through the streets and roads of Northern New York.

The Advance's headline blared:

BOOTLEGGERS HAILING WITH JOY REPORT OF GRAND JURY REC- OMMENDING TROOPER SPINKS BE REMOVED FOR SHOOTING BOOTLEGGER, FINDS NO INDICTMENT AGAINST CAPTAIN HOLLAND OR TROOPER SPINKS FOR THE KILLING

The St. Lawrence County Grand Jury on Saturday, at the close of its work, announced that it had failed to indict Henry Holland, collector of customs of the Port of Ogdensburg, and Trooper Charles Spinks of the state police for the killing of Wilbur P. Hunt, a boot- legger, following a pursuit of the bootlegger's car. The grand jury condemned the act and asked that Trooper Spinks be dismissed.[60]

"The action of the grand jury, in recommending Spinks' dis- missal, will meet the approval of every bootlegger in the county," the Advance's Editor and Publisher George Darrow wrote. "The peo- ple are asking: if Spinks must go, what about Holland, under whose direction the chase was made?"

The report is as follows: Court House, Canton, N.Y., Jan. 22, 1922. To Honorable Henry V. Borst, Justice of the Supreme Court of the State of New York:

Dear Sir—The undersigned Grand Jurors of the Court of St. Law- rence after deliberating many hours on the case of the People vs. Henry Holland and Charles Spinks, charged with manslaughter in the first degree, have finally decided that no indictment should be had.

However, the grand jury does not feel that it can overlook the killing of a human being on the public highway in the County of St. Lawrence in the manner in which the life of Wilbur Hunt was taken,

---

[60] Ogdensburg Advance and Weekly St. Lawrence Democrat, Jan. 26, 1922

and stating their views in some way, so that the public may have some idea as to their position, after hearing the evidence in this very important case.

We are absolutely opposed to the illegal traffic in intoxicating liquors, and desire to suppress as far as possible the said traffic, and we are willing to stand back of the officers of the law in the prosecution of their duty.

We do not feel, however, that it was necessary to take a human life in this instance. We feel that the officers felt that they were performing their duty, but in the view of the testimony which has been given before the Grand Jury, and which is clear. It is our recommendation that Trooper Charles Spinks of the State Police of the State of New York, is unfit for the position which he occupies and should be dismissed from the service. First, the public highways must be always kept safe for the travel of our citizens, men, women and children, and greater care must be exercised by the officers in cases of this kind.

We respectfully ask that this recommendation be sent to the commanding officer of the State Police of the State of New York and that this statement be given for publication.

Advance Editor Darrow was outraged by the Grand Jury's suggestion that the Trooper Spinks ought to be punished and removed from the state police for daring to protect the people of the state from criminals and performing his duty at the risk of his own life.

"There is no doubt that every bootlegger in the state would like to see such men as Trooper Spinks removed from the force," Darrow wrote. "They fear a man who can shoot straight and who is not afraid to face a gun in the hands of a running bootlegger. According to a report from Malone there is no likelihood of Major Chandler removing Spinks. To do so would be a blot upon the law's enforcement. It was only a few weeks ago that the Franklin County Board of Supervisors passed a resolution asking for an investigation into the acts of certain state troopers in giving the third degree to some suspected "rum runners." The Franklin County District Attorney held an investigation and found the charges unsubstantiated. The people of Malone held a mass meeting which was attended by hundreds at which time the action of the supervisors was condemned. It is so in this case. The people who believe in the constitution and the law's enforcement are behind Trooper Spinks to a man. They know that bootleggers will not stop at the wave of a hand from an official. No matter if the few men composing the grand jury recommend a laxity in enforcing the war against whiskey runners, the people will still demand that our county and state officials continue to do their duty.

The reaction to the Grand Jury's decision varied across the region, depending on people's views on law enforcement and whether people favored the Prohibition laws.

In the Feb. 14, 1922, edition of Ogdensburg's Republican Journal, the editors decided to offer coverage of a fiery sermon from a Potsdam Baptist Church, even though it criticized their editorials that condemned the shooting of the bootleggers and supported prosecuting the U.S. Customs Collector and the New York State Trooper.

POTSDAM, Feb. 13—The general topic of law enforcement and the situation along the Northern border was the subject of a sermon at the Baptist Church Sunday evening by Rev. A. H. McKnight, pastor of the church. McKnight's discourse has aroused great interest, referring to the case of Trooper Spinks of the state constabulary who shot and killed W. F. Hunt, a Watertown bootlegger last fall and to the attitude in the case of District Attorney W. D. Ingram.[61]

---

[61] Ogdensburg Republican Journal, Feb. 14, 1921

POTSDAM BAPTIST CHURCH AND PARSONAGE

BORDER TOPIC OF POTSDAM MLNISTER'S SERMON DECLARES TROOPER SPINKS JUSTIFIED IN FIRING SHOT THAT KILLED HUNT- MALONE PETITION FOR REMOVAL OF TROOPERS CRITICIZED

The question of lack of cooperation between the various divisions of the law enforcement officers was cited by the pastor who also referred to the petition made up in Malone for the removal of the troopers from that village.

Cites Abraham Lincoln

Rev. McKnight took his text from an address of Abraham Lincoln, the service being a Lincoln service: Let reverence for law be the political religion of the Nation.

Rev. McKnight said in part: Now as to the case of Trooper Spinks, I do not know Trooper Spinks. I do not know that I have ever seen him. But he is an officer of the law. He is commissioned to apprehend law breakers. In the early part of October, Collector of Customs Holland, of Ogdensburg received a tip that a load of bootleg liquor was "coming through."

There are two things we need to keep in mind regarding bootlegging. First, those engaged are breaking three laws: the Volstead Act of the national government, the Mullan-Gage law of the state of New York and in addition they are smugglers. Second, those engaged in trafficking are criminals. The fact of the matter is that many of them are dangerous criminals. Most of them are gunmen.

Tonight, officers apprehended the bootlegging smugglers near Old Dekalb. The officers were in uniform. The smugglers could not but have known that they were officers of the law. Instead of stopping when they were commanded to, they endeavored to make a getaway. And in a running fight, Trooper Spinks, who was standing on the running board, and fully exposed to the bootlegger's gun, shot, and killed Wilbur F. Hunt of Watertown.

HUNT UNDER INDICTMENT

And who was Hunt? A veteran bootlegger. A man mixed up a short time before in a shooting affair of bootleggers in Carthage. A man under indictment and out on bail. It does not matter who he was. At this time, he was committing a crime. The following things happened. Trooper Spinks and Collector Holland were arrested and charged with manslaughter upon the action of the district attorney. I do not know the district attorney, but he seems to be a very zealous man, at least in certain directions, and particularly as regards officers of the law. Some people took a strange position regarding the affair. The press of the North Country took a stand that was commendable. Every paper, except two, (the Gouverneur Tribune Press and the Ogdensburg Republican Journal) stood by the enforcement of law.

They stood fore square for Spinks and Holland. One said that

Spinks should be given a pension. Another said that Holland should be given a gold medal.

CRITICIZES JURORS' LETTER

The matter was brought before the Grand Jury at Canton recently and neither Spinks nor Holland were indicted. Unfortunately, the Grand Jury wrote a letter to New York State Supreme Court Justice Borst recommending the dismissal of Trooper Spinks, which letter, I take it, was forwarded to Major Chandler, the head of the New York State Police in Albany who treated it as a joke.

This letter is a very peculiar statement. Our Grand jury declares a man innocent and then asks for his dismissal. Do we get a different type of trooper up this way?

BORDER PATROL BADGE (PUBLIC DOMAIN)

I have known of the troopers ever since they were organized, and I have never known of any serious complaint against them by any law-abiding citizen. The trouble with the state troopers is that they stop lawlessness that some other officers have long winked at. Some groups of men, Masonic; fair association, some fire companies, some lodges, some church men want to pull off certain gambling stunts. Some big man in town wants to race his car through the streets. Somebody wants to make home brew and pass it out. Everybody counts one and only one with the troopers. That is where the problem is. Men like Hunt are not the worst criminals, though he was a despised outlaw. The worst type are those intelligent, respectable people, so-called, that exhibit a disregard for law. Particularly if it is a law that interferes with something they would like to do.

TROOPER CHARLES SPINKS RESIGNED, JOINED BORDER PATROL

Two years later, the Lake Placid News reported that Trooper Charles Spinks had decided to leave the New York State Police. But the news did not cheer up the North Country's bootleggers and smugglers when they learned the deadly shot had only traded in his state police badge for the one issued by the newly formed U.S. Border Patrol which had been created by Congress to specifically guard the border and assist in the crackdown on smugglers and bootleggers.[62]

Announcement of the appointment of Charles Spinks, formerly a member of the State Constabulary (state police) to the U. S. Border Patrol under command of Capt. F. S. Steinberg of Malone, recalled the fact that he was one of the chief figures in the Wilbur Hunt shooting case at Old Dekalb, Oct. 12, 1921. Hunt, who came from Watertown, was one of the occupants of a liquor laden car which was being pursued by a party of federal officers and state troopers headed by U.S. Customs Collector Henry Holland.

---

[62] Lake Placid News, Dec. 4, 1924

It was said at the time that the bootleggers were about to fire at the officers' car when Trooper Spinks, who was standing on the running board, discharged his revolver.

Hunt was struck in the chin and instantly killed.

The shooting caused a big sensation, and public opinion was divided into groups, one contending that the shooting was justifiable while the other held that it was not.

District Attorney W. D. Ingram of St. Lawrence County hauled both Collector Holland and Trooper Spinks into court on charges of manslaughter in the first degree and they were held for the grand jury.

No indictments were found but the jury handed up a statement addressed to Judge Borst of the Supreme Court, who presided.

Spinks remained in the service of the state police and was only recently promoted to sergeant.

He was stationed this fall at Lowville, but it is said he got into a disagreement with Captain Broadfield over the order which does not allow a married trooper to reside with his wife on outpost duty. Spinks married a Malone girl a few weeks ago and it is reported that because he could not take her with him to Lowville, he resigned and sought admission to the U.S. Border Patrol.

Spinks has been regarded as one of the most active troopers along the border and has accounted for seizures of hundreds of booze cars in the St. Lawrence River section.

When U.S. Customs Collector J. C. Tulloch learned Trooper Spinks wished to join the U.S. Border Patrol, he said the matter would be given immediate attention. He said that Spinks had received the highest recommendations for his new job. Spinks comes from Fayetteville.

Moonshine Still (Wikimedia Commons)

CHAPTER 14

NEVER BRING AN AX TO A HOLIDAY DANCE & OTHER SECOND WARD TIPS

Call it one of the most important unwritten rules of hosting a party in Ogdensburg's colorful Second Ward neighborhoods at the turn of the century.

It was true 100 years ago during the Prohibition era.

It is still good advice today.

Never bring an ax to a Christmas dance.

William Dishaw broke the rule during a holiday party he hosted in 1921.

It cost him a successful career making illegal 200-proof moonshine for his Pine Street neighbors.

The neighborhood had come together to enjoy a holiday dance at his 88 Pine Street home that featured Dishaw's finest 16-week aged corn mash whiskey, but when the 43-year-old liquor maker drank so much of his own holiday recipe that he went into an ax wielding rage, his guests and relatives worried someone might end up hurt.[63]

When he staggered next door to his son-in-law's home and began smashing the door, windows and even the stove with his ax, one of

---

[63] Ogdensburg Republican Journal, Dec. 19, 1921

his guests, William Brenno, decided it was time to take extreme measures, calling the Ogdensburg Police Department to ask for help.

City police officers Amo, McDonald and Farley confronted the drunken 43-year-old party host, ordering him to drop the ax and accompany them back to a downtown cell where he could sleep off his high-test holiday spirits.

When Dishaw refused, and began running away, Officer Farley pulled his pistol and fired a warning shot in the air, according to a newspaper story on the incident reported in the Dec. 19th, 1921, edition of the Ogdensburg Republican Journal.

Brenno, who was out on bail for harboring a criminal, saw that his drunk neighbor was provoking the police officers who were concerned that the liquored-up ax wielding Dishaw might really ruin the Christmas spirit by maiming or killing a guest or even a family member.

Brenno worried if Dishaw refused to surrender, one of the police officers might shoot him if he felt he was endangering the lives of his guests or the police.

After Officer Farley fired the warning shot, Dishaw made a motion as if he were reaching for a concealed gun. Brenno tackled him and brought him to the floor, where officers were able to help subdue him and handcuff him.

City police praised Brenno for his bravery, acknowledging that by risking his own life, he had saved Dishaw from being shot.

The following day, when District Attorney William Ingram consulted with the Ogdensburg Police about the evening's events, they had a courageous story about the efforts of brave-hearted police and a courageous citizen who risked his own life to prevent what could have turned into a senseless holiday tragedy.

But as Ogdensburg Police and St. Lawrence County District Attorney William Ingram began reviewing charges against Dishaw, they discovered he offered more than just a simple case of a drunken host wielding an ax during a Christmas Party.

The unlucky Dishaw offered Ogdensburg police and the DA a terrific opportunity to show that the Maple City's law enforcement community was cracking down on the illicit booze traffic.

The District Attorney and the entire Ogdensburg Police Department had been under repeated public attack in newspapers across St. Lawrence County and the entire state of New York for their abject failure to arrest people connected with the illicit rum smuggling and speakeasy operations in Ogdensburg.

With Democrat newspaper editors like George Darrow arguing in the pages of the Ogdensburg Advance and Weekly St. Lawrence Democrat that the young Republican prosecutor and the Ogdensburg police force had failed to even make an attempt to run the demon rum runners out of the Maple City, Dishaw provided them with a perfect example of their new found zeal to crack down on the illicit liquor trade.

The Dec. 19th, 1921, edition of the Ogdensburg Republican Journal recorded the shining example of how Ogdensburg and St. Lawrence County officials were working together to crack down on the liquor trade:

MOONSHINER CAUGHT AFTER CHASE, STILL AND HOOCH REMOVED
AFTER DISHAW GOES ON A RAMPAGE DURING DANCE
— WILLIE BRENNO, OUT ON BAIL, HIMSELF DOWNS FUGITIVE

William Dishaw, 43, of 88 Pine Street was arrested Saturday by Police Officers McDonald, Farley, and Amo and locked up on a charge of making moonshine liquor.

The police confiscated a still and several gallons of hooch.[64]

Most importantly city police and Ingram made sure the story was reported in lurid detail in the pages of the Palmer brothers and A.E. Sansoucy's GOP friendly "Ogdensburg Republican Journal."

The newspaper reported police, and the District Attorney discovered a moonshine still Dishaw used to produce liquor that he had cleverly hidden inside a hole under the kitchen floor of a vacant house at 84 Pine Street.

Several gallons of pure 200 proof Maple City Moonshine was found hidden at 86 Pine Street where Dishaw's son-in-law, a man named O'Brien lived.

O'Brien denied any knowledge of how the moonshine had gotten into his house or the location of his father-in-law's still.

District Attorney Ingram boasted to the newspaper that the arrest of the moonshiner represented one of the most significant examples of the city's crackdown on illegal booze in Ogdensburg. During his arraignment, Dishaw admitted he owned the still and had been making liquor with it. He was held on $2,000 bail.

"The police believe that Dishaw has been in the moonshine game for some time and has been peddling the stuff in the Pine Street district. The ax Dishaw used was found Saturday afternoon by Officer Nicholson, who with District Attorney Ingram, visited the scene and searched the premises. The ax was taken to police headquarters. A wooden tub filled with corn mash, said to be 16 days (about 2 and a half weeks)-old, was also found and brought to police headquarters.

"Members of Dishaw's family told the District Attorney they were afraid of him and after visiting the premises and surveying the wreck, the District Attorney said it was a wonder that Dishaw had

---

[64] Ogdensburg Republican Journal, Dec. 19, 1921

not maimed somebody during his rampage. The police said the confiscated moonshine packed a 100 percent kick.

CORRUPT STATE POLICE SERGEANT CAUGHT HIJACKING LIQUOR

HOGANSBURG - When a uniformed New York State Police Sergeant was caught confiscating a load of booze near Hogansburg on the St. Regis Reservation, he insisted he had the authority as a trooper to conduct his own one-man raid, even without authorization or the awareness of his superiors 120 south in Oneida, N.Y.[65]

But when authorities questioned just who the trooper was, they discovered he had driven 120 miles north from Oneida, near Utica, on his own time, without authorization from his superiors or anyone else in the state police.

When he was detained by federal authorities who questioned under whose authority he was confiscating loads of illicit liquor, the trooper claimed he intended to turn over the booze to the U.S. Custom House in Malone.

He told a federal justice in Auburn that he was not trying to confiscate the liquor for himself to sell illegally. Instead, he argued that he decided to take a leave of absence from his actual official duties to travel north to the international border to demonstrate his sense of initiative in the hope of winning a promotion. He intercepted a load of liquor being delivered to the American side of the St. Regis Reservation.

Federal officers asked the federal grand jury at Binghamton to

---

[65] Malone Farmer, July 20, 1921

indict him for illegal possession of liquor. He was held on $1,000 bond.

The trooper was charged with a crime before U. S. Commissioner Lawrence in Malone at the insistence of Deputy Director John W. Bert of Hogansburg, who placed him under arrest.

He was discharged for lack of sufficient evidence to hold him with the understanding that the evidence would be handed over to the U.S. Attorney for such action as he might decide. The formal accusation is the result. Bright was suspended from the State police force following his arrest pending a disposal of the case, and Major Chandler refused to reinstate him because he wore his uniform when not on duty.

GOUVERNEURIANS DISTURBED BY RUM RUNNERS LOCAL POLICE OFFICERS WATCH THEM WHIZ PAST, PAPER SAYS.

The April 11th edition of the Ogdensburg Republican Journal observed the current issue of a Gouverneur paper carried the following interesting item: GOUVERNEUR - "Every morning early risers among the residents of West Main Street see speed laws badly shaken on that thoroughfare by west bound booze runners who pass by with high-powered cars at a speed of from 35 to 50 miles per hour, all heavily laden with Canadian liquor. [66]

The great speed kept seems useless in view of the- fact that no one seems to be inclined to interfere with them in this section. All local officers are under the impression that they have no right to arrest traffickers in liquor and they just sit on the fence and watch them pass with full loads.

Most of the bootleggers pass through here between the hours of

---

[66] Ogdensburg Republican Journal, April 11, 1921

3 and 6 in the morning, although numbers get through during the day and many of them stop for lunch and gasoline, according to the reports of bystanders."

State Troopers Found Rum Runners Would Kill to Smuggle Booze

CHAPTER 15

BOOTLEGGER ATTEMPTED
TO KILL HELPLESS TROOPER

New York State Trooper Frederick A. Waterman lay on the cold late November ground, writhing in pain, his knee shattered.[67]

The angry smuggler aimed the revolver at the lawman's heart. He had wrestled the gun away from the trooper during the struggle which had ended when the weapon discharged, the bullet striking the state police officer in his leg.

Bootlegger Charles Lajoie aimed the revolver at Waterman's heart, preparing to pull the trigger.

The lawman saw his death reflected in the eyes of the bootlegger.

The revolver clicked as the Montreal man pulled the trigger in an angry rage, but the weapon did not fire.

The six shots had been discharged during the chase and struggle.

Furious, Lajoi began pistol-whipping the trooper, leaving the lawman's face a swollen, bloody mess.

Worried that the state police officer's partner might arrive at any time, Lajoie and his partner, Alexander Boyer, fled.

The night had begun when acting on a tip from U.S. Customs

---

[67] Chateaugay Record and Franklin County Democrat, Nov. 25, 1921

men, Trooper Waterman and Corporal A. Newing began patrolling the road near Mooers Forks on the watch for two loads of whiskey believed due to pass over the highway.

Midway between Starks and Whitley Corners they saw a Locomobile and Cadillac car approach.

The leading machine sighted the troopers in their Ford and turned into a dirt road running across the country and leading to another main thoroughfare that would have led them back to safety in Canada. The troopers drew up on the fleeing cars. Seeing that capture was unavoidable the men ditched their machines and started running.

Corporal Newing soon overtook Alexander Verdo and James Powers, also of Montreal, who had separated from the other two men.

They submitted to arrest without a struggle.

Waterman had taken after the other two who had run in a different direction. Calling upon them to halt and seeing his command disobeyed, the trooper fired, striking Lajoie in the hand. Lajoie halted and as the trooper approached him, grappled with him. Lajoie sought to take the officer's gun from him. During the scuffle, the revolver discharged, the bullet shattering Waterman's knee and breaking the big bone of the leg.

Gaining possession of the revolver, Lajoie pressed the weapon against the helpless trooper's heart and pulled the trigger. Fortunately, the gun was empty. Enraged, the Canadian smashed the trooper about the face with butt of the revolver until the lawman's face was cut and bruised.

Leaving Waterman lying helpless on the ground, blood flowing from his leg and face and suffering intense pain, the two Canadian bootleggers dashed on into the woods hoping to make their escape. Newing soon arrived at his companion's side and got Waterman to a farmhouse where medical aid was secured, and arrangements made to remove the injured trooper to a hospital in Plattsburgh.

Corporal Newing notified Malone headquarters and Captain Charles J. Broadfield, troop commander, with a squad of men, took to the field bent on apprehending those who had tried to kill a brother officer. Orders went out in every direction and a drag net was drawn close about the section in which the fight occurred.

Troopers were ordered to get the men at any cost.

Picking up the trail at the scene of the fight, Captain Broadfield and his men traced Lajoie and Boyer to the home of Wilbur Bedor, four miles distant. Surrounding the house, the captain rapped at the door and asked if the fugitives were there. Bedor admitted they were. Captain Broadfield, with a sergeant, rushed into the house and had the men in cuffs before they could offer resistance.

The prisoners were all taken to Plattsburgh and arraigned before U.S. Commissioner H. P. Gilliland.

Doctors fear that Trooper Waterman may have to have one leg amputated above the knee because of the shattering of the kneecap by the bullet.

Trooper Shot in Gun Battle
2 Booze Laden Cars Seized Near Malone, 60 Cases of Liquor and 3rd Car Taken Carrying Revolvers but Without Liquor at Hogansburg

MALONE, Dec. 1 - When New York State Trooper J. Carroll was shot by a fleeing bootlegger not far from Malone during a running gun battle in a high speed chase near the Canadian border, the public saw once again that officers were risking their lives in the increasingly violent battle to stop the liquor flowing across the border from Canada. [68]

---

[68] Ogdensburg Republican Journal, Dec. 1, 1921

U.S. Customs officer Reed demonstrated that the federal inspectors assigned to the Northern border were just as fearless as the men being recruited for the New York State Police when he leaped from his vehicle to the running board of the vehicle, he and his colleagues were pursuing across Northern Franklin County.

Customs Officers Reed and Willard King and State Troopers Carroll and Benning had picked up the trail of a booze car at a point northwest of Malone. The officers ordered the driver of the car to stop but he did not obey the order and attempted to get away.

Customs Officer Reed jumped on the running board of the speeding car and ordered the driver to stop.

Instead of doing so, the smuggler stepped on the speed in an all-out effort to dislodge King, who clung to the car in a desperate effort to get the driver to stop. Finally, Customs Officer King drew his revolver and ordered the driver to stop the car or face the consequences of his efforts to endanger his fellow Customs officer who could have been killed in the high-speed chase.

The car was occupied by a woman and child besides the driver.

The other cruisers, including the state troopers, were in the thick of the chase after seeing the car refuse to pull over.

State Trooper J. Carroll was wounded in the right ankle by a bullet fired by an occupant of one of the fleeing booze laden cars.

Trooper Carroll was rushed to Alice Hyde Hospital in Malone after the shooting for treatment, but fortunately, doctors say, the wound was not too serious, and a quick recovery is expected.

In the roundup, sixty cases of liquor, including both whiskey and beer were seized by the officials, together with a new Cadillac roadster and a truck, both of which were loaded with booze.

Two men in a third car were taken into custody with the car on a charge of having concealed weapons in their possession without a license.

The occupants of the captured car gave their names as Joseph Kinnetville of Rochester, along with his wife and child. They were driving a new Cadillac Roadster which was loaded with twenty-seven cases of liquor, including several brands of whiskey. The Cadillac and the occupants of the car with the captured booze were all brought to Malone in the custody of the officials.

While the seizure of the Cadillac was in progress another party of officials, including Customs Officers Harpur and Deputy Edwards, Franklin County Sheriff Steenberge and State Troopers Ford, Canfield, Jackson and McCreedy were busy preparing for the coming of a booze car and had arranged so it would be difficult for the car to get by.

The officers did not have long to wait. Once the Booze car came to the obstruction the driver turned sharply into a gap going along on its side but did not turn over. The occupants of the car were Italians and said they were from Rochester. The car did not have liquor, but officers said they believed the occupants were on their way to get a load.

One of the occupants of the car was thrown out during their attempt to escape and went under the icy waters of Deer River. He was frightened and after the officers rescued him, he declared he had drowned because he thought his lungs had filled with water.

Dr. MacArtney of Fort Covington was called and when he arrived on the scene at the river, he took measures to get the water out of the Italian's lungs and he was found to be no worse for his experience though drenched to the skin from his immersion in the river.

Sheriff Steenberg took into custody two Italians from Utica who were carrying concealed weapons.

While the thrilling high speed gun battle and shooting of a New York State trooper might have been expected to impress the residents of Malone with the bravery and daring of the officers assigned to protect the Northern border, newspaper readers across the state were shocked when they discovered that the incident had caused an entirely different reaction among some.

NEW YORK STATE POLICE WAR ON BOOTLEGGERS

CHAPTER 16

TROOPERS RISK LIVES, BUT FACE CRITICS

When the New York State Police announced plans to locate their barracks in Malone, the community celebrated the arrival of the 50 plus "Grey Riders." But as the law enforcement officers began enforcing the dry laws, searching, and seizing vehicles, and even engaging in gunfights with armed thugs who were intent on thumbing their noses at Prohibition, the officers discovered their jobs were dangerous and the criminals they hunted had no regard for whether the troopers lived or died.

TROOPER SHOT BY ROCHESTER HOOD WHO BROUGHT WIFE, CHILD
TROOPER SHOT, SIX ARRESTED IN DRY RAID, RED LETTER DAY FOR NORTH IN ENFORCMENT OF BOOZE LAW – BABY IS PRISONER

The shooting of a state trooper in a skirmish with alleged bootleggers last Thursday, the arrest of six persons, one a woman with an infant in her arms, the seizure of 60 cases of liquor worth $6,000, the confiscation of three autos and the sinking of a fourth in the Deer River along the Canadian border line near Fort Covington, all contributed to making a red letter day in the annals of law enforcement in the

North and one not soon to be forgotten by a score of Federal and state officers who played leading roles in the scenes enacted.[69]

Officers declared Trooper Carrol was fired upon by the occupant of a vehicle driven by Joe Kenevllle, of Rochester, whose wife and baby were riding with him.

A search of Keneville's car and its occupants, halted only after a desperate attempt was made by the driver to evade capture, failed to reveal the gun used to shoot the trooper.

Twenty-eight cases of Scotch whiskey were taken during the seizure of Keneville's machine. He carried both Quebec and New York license plates; the former being attached to the car at the time of its capture.

Customs Inspector Willard King was given a thrilling ride for several hundred feet before Kenevllle finally halted. But only after the Customs Inspector pressed the muzzle of his gun against the smuggler.

King leaped onto the running board of the vehicle only to have Keneville attempt to shake the federal officer from the running board of his fleeing car without success. Troopers Carroll, Deming and Customs Officer Reed aided King in making the capture.

At the same time as the Keneville episode was being enacted, Franklin County Sheriff Steenberger, Customs Officers Stark and Harmon and Troopers Ford, Jackson, Canfield and Mccreedy we're having their share of difficulties in capturing a second car. This was a truck loaded with 30 cases of liquor and was by men who gave their names as John Doyle and Henry Roberts of Buffalo.

Seeing the roadway ahead of them blocked with the vehicles of the officers, the smugglers swerved the truck into a field, leaving the

---

[69] Chateaugay Record, Dec. 9, 1921

highway and pursuing a course through the field until their escape was blocked by a brook.

Unable to ford this with the truck, they leaped out and ran for a wooded area near at hand. They surrendered when the officers threatened to fire into the clump of trees in which they were hiding. The officers covered four miles of territory in the high-speed chase before the men were captured.

Later, in the night while the search for liquor laden machines was still being carried on, Sheriff Steenberger came upon another vehicle driven by two men identified as Rocco V. Marrone and Charles C. Coupe, both of Utica.

Search of the machine did not reveal any contraband liquor, but the sheriff uncovered a revolver from one man who had a defective permit.

The men were arrested on a charge of carrying concealed weapons.

No attachment will be made to the car.

It will be turned back to the men when the other matter has been adjusted. It was declared merely a technicality existed regarding the permit. Both entered pleas of not guilty when charged before Magistrate Moses Burno and asked for an examination.

The night brought about another successful raid when officers visited the St. Regis Mohawk Indian reservation at Hogansburg and made Dan Lazore, an Indian, a captive. A warrant was held for his arrest following a raid made upon his premises on Sunday, when 200 quarts of ale and beer were confiscated. Lazore was taken into custody while trying to escape by way of a roof.

Two Italians, who claimed homes in Rochester, narrowly escaped drowning in the Deer River near Fort Covington when their machine did not negotiate a turn and plunged into the river. It partly turned on its side but did not turn completely over.

It was just after the accident took place that the officers came upon the machine. They rescued the men from the water, finding it necessary to apply resuscitation methods to one of them, whose lungs had filled with water and who was near death.

ROCHESTER HOOD WHO SHOT STATE TROOPER FINED $450

UTICA - The United States District Court at Utica Judge Ray imposed a fine of $450 upon Joseph Keneville of Rochester for violation of the National Prohibition act in the possession and transportation of liquor. The charge against Mrs. Keneville who was with her husband, who was held for the grand jury on a similar charge, was not pressed in court in Utica.[70]

Keneville was also indicted by the Grand Jury for an alleged attempt to bribe a government officer. He has given bond for his appearance in federal court to answer the charge.

Keneville and his wife were arrested on Nov. 30 by Malone federal and local officers on a highway northwest of Malone.

They were driving a Cadillac roadster which was loaded "with twenty-seven cases of Canadian liquor. The allegation that Keneville was brutally treated by the officers following his arrest provoked calls for an investigation into the state police's treatment of the smugglers and bootleggers who tried to kill them.

---

[70] Ogdensburg Republican Journal, Dec. 19, 1921

New York State Police Founder George F. Chandler Refused to Pull His Troopers Out of Malone Despite Demands from Attorneys and Smugglers

CONSPIRACY AGAINST TROOPERS? INVESTIGATION IS DEMANDED IN FRANKLIN COUNTY; LAWYERS WANT TROOPERS OUT

The Dec. 27, 1921, edition of the Ogdensburg Journal reported a delegation of lawyers appeared before the Franklin County Board of Supervisors to present a petition asking the state to remove Troop B from the North Country.

The headline reported:

MALONE BOARD OF SUPERVISORS WANT TROOPERS PULLED OUT DELEGATION OF LAWYERS APPEAR BEFORE THE SUPERVISORS AND PETITION BOARD TO REQUEST THE REMOVAL OF STATE POLICE FROM MALONE
— WARRANTS DENIED BY JUDGE PADDOCK IN KENEVILLE CASE

MALONE - When a contingent of lawyers appeared before the Franklin County Board of Supervisors a few days after Christmas in 1921, asking their elected officials to request the removal of the State Police's Black Horse Brigade from Malone, it showed not everyone was thrilled with what it meant to crack down on the North Country's fastest growing industry - illegal booze running.[71]

Supervisor Payne introduced a resolution before the Franklin County Board of Supervisors asking Major Chandler to conduct an investigation into the "unlawful acts performed and committed by Troop B since their location in Malone, and that a copy of the resolution be transmitted to Major Chandler with "the request that such an investigation be conducted at an early date."

Members of the Franklin County Bar Association appeared with a petition prepared for presentation to the Board formally requesting the removal of Troop B from Malone.

Following considerable informal discussion, the petition was withdrawn by the lawyers, as being too drastic and impractical, and later the above resolution was adopted by the Board.

Franklin County Judge Frederick G. Paddock Saturday made his report in the matter of the investigation of alleged brutal treatment of Joseph Keneville of Rochester, by officials at the entrance and inside the Franklin County jail following Keneville's arrest for whiskey running on the night of November 30th.

The investigation was requested by the members of the Franklin County Board of Supervisors in a letter addressed to District Attorney E. C. Lawrence.

Franklin County District Attorney Lawrence conducted the investigation before Judge Paddock, calling witnesses who testified with their versions of what they said happened after the Rochester man was brought to the Franklin County jail after he was arrested for smuggling liquor across the border.

Judge Paddock ruled that after hearing the accounts of Paddock

---

[71] Ogdensburg Republican Journal, Dec. 27, 1921

and eyewitnesses who offered conflicting accounts: "I have carefully examined the evidence and the same is so conflicting, contradictory and uncertain, and there is so much disagreement "as to what actually occurred, I do not think it is sufficient to overcome the presumption of innocence and the benefit of the doubt which must be given to anyone charged with a crime, and therefore I decline" to recommend that anyone be charged in connection with the case.

ASK REMOVAL OF STATE POLICE, FRANKLIN COUNTY LAWYERS AFTERWARDS AMEND RESOLUTION, HULLABALOO BEFORE SUPERVISORS

There is something of a furor in Malone just now over the state police question. Several members of the Franklin County Bar appeared before the board of supervisors Friday at their closing session and presented a petition asking for the removal of Troop B from Malone.[72]

Following considerable informal discussions of the matter, the petition was withdrawn as being too drastic and impractical and the supervisors adopted the following resolution: "Resolved, in view of the complaints of a large number of citizens of Franklin County as to the unlawful acts performed and committed by Troop B of the State Constabulary, located at Malone, that Maj. Chandler be requested to conduct an investigation of the conduct.

200 MALONE MEN STAND WITH TROOPERS GO ON RECORD TO COMMEND THEM

Two hundred or more Malone men have "placed themselves on record supporting the work of members of Troop B, state police

---

[72] Courier Freeman, Potsdam, Dec. 28, 1921

whose headquarters are in Malone. A petition was recently presented to the board of supervisors asking for removal of the troop. This was later withdrawn. And the supervisors finally passed a resolution asking Major Chandler, head of the state constabulary, to investigate the conduct since the troop was set up.[73]

Judge Frederick Paddock, county judge of Franklin County, addressed the members of the Benefit Club, a men's club of Malone a few days ago and warmly defended the troopers.

In his speech, Judge Paddock told the clubmen that if they believed in law and order and in its enforcement then they must lend their efforts to the state police despite recent efforts to blacken their character.

If, on the other hand, the men believed in whiskey running, narcotic smuggling and other forms of crime that have prevailed in the border country, they should join the street critics who circulate falsehoods about the troopers.

Following the address a resolution was passed stating that the members of the Benefit Club would support the state police in every way possible in their fight to stamp out crime along the Canadian border.

A copy of this resolution was ordered sent to Major George F. Chandler.

STATE POLICE CAPTAIN CHARACTERIZES REQUEST FOR PROBE: WORK OF FRIENDS OF BOOTLEGGERS

MALONE - Capt. Broadfield of the State troopers stationed at Malone, believes that the request for an investigation of the acts of members of the Troop is the result of agitation of

---

[73] Courier Freeman, Potsdam, Jan. 4, 1922

friends of the liquor traffic and sympathizers with bootleggers, "if they can arouse public opinion against us," says the captain, "and blacken the reputation of our organization or bring us into general disrespect with the people of this territory, it is to their advantage. Reports have been heard that we were to be driven out of here. That is impossible but the criminal element would surely be glad to get rid of us.[74]

U.S. Customs Claims War Victory on War on Rum at End Of 1922, But Prohibition, Rumrunning

At the end of 1922, U.S. Customs Collector Henry Holland insisted his officers were winning, despite the articles in metropolitan papers that were painting a much different picture to the effect that liquor smugglers were finding it easy to ply their illicit business along the northern border.

Holland offered a detailed summary of the arrests and seizures made in the Ogdensburg Customs District which stretched 250 miles from Rouses Point to Oswego.

"During the past year, 372 seizures of liquor have been made in this district and 106 automobiles, in variety from a Pierce-Arrow to a Ford, were confiscated, together with 20 horses, four motor launches, 54 tons of hay and 41,159-quart bottles of whiskey. Upwards of 500 arrests have been made and fines imposed ranging from $400 to $1,000 each. There are about 12 roads to every mile in this territory and the customs force is only sufficient for the office and inspection work.

"Notwithstanding the fact that newspaper correspondents assert that large quantities of liquor have been smuggled across, it is inti-

---

[74] Courier Freeman, Potsdam, Jan. 11, 1921

mated that two-thirds of the liquor that crossed the international line in this territory was seized by government officers. Whiskey has been found in every conceivable hiding place, including carloads of hay, boats, automobiles, trucks, pulpwood, potatoes, secreted in butter, Christmas trees, fish boxes, steel drums and wagons."

Prohibition continued for 11 more years until it was repealed in 1933.

CITATIONS

1 Ogdensburg Republican Journal, Oct. 23, 1921

2 Ogdensburg Republican Journal, Oct. 24, 1921

3 Ogdensburg Advance and Weekly Democrat, Oct. 25, 1921

4 Ogdensburg Republican Journal, Oct. 25, 1921

5 Ogdensburg, Republican Journal, Oct. 27, 1921

6 Ogdensburg Advance and Weekly Democrat, Jan. 6, 1921

7 Canton Commercial Advertiser, Jan. 11, 1921

8 Potsdam Courier Freeman, Jan. 12, 1921

9 Ogdensburg Republican Journal, Jan. 13, 1921

10 Ogdensburg Republican Journal, Jan. 13, 1921

11 Massena Observer, Jan. 6, 1921

12 Ogdensburg Republican Journal, Jan. 12, 1921

13 Republican Journal, Oct. 21, 1921

14 Republican Journal, Jan. 14, 1921

15 Ogdensburg Republican Journal, Jan. 17, 1921

16 Ogdensburg Republican Journal, Jan. 21, 1921

17 The Republican Journal, Ogdensburg, Feb. 10, 1921

18 Advance News, Sept. 7, 1975 (Interview with Jimmy Brenno 50 years after the incident)

19 Ogdensburg Republican Journal, Feb. 16, 1921

20 Ogdensburg Republican Journal, Feb. 11, 1921

21 Ogdensburg Advance News, Sept. 7, 1975

22 Ogdensburg Republican Journal, Feb. 11, 1921

23 Advance News, Sept. 7, 1975

24 Ogdensburg Republican Journal, Feb. 10, 1921

25 Syracuse Post Standard, Feb. 14, 1921

26 Ogdensburg Republican Journal, Feb. 15, 1921

27 Ogdensburg Republican Journal, Feb. 15, 1921

28 Ogdensburg Republican Journal, Feb. 15, 1921

29 Ogdensburg Republican Journal, Feb. 15, 1921

30 Ogdensburg Republican Journal, Feb. 16, 1921

31 Ogdensburg Republican Journal, Feb. 26, 1921

32 Ogdensburg Republican Journal, Feb. 26, 1921

33 Ogdensburg Republican Journal, Feb. 18, 1921

34 Ogdensburg Republican Journal, June 9, 1921

35 Advance News, Ogdensburg, Sept. 7, 1975 (Interview with Jimmy Brenno 50 years after incident)

36 Ogdensburg Republican Journal, Oct. 17, 1921

37 Ogdensburg Advance and Weekly St. Lawrence Democrat

38 Massena Observer, March 17, 1921

39 Massena Observer, March 24, 1921

40 Ogdensburg Republican Journal, Feb. 25, 1921

41 Ogdensburg Republican Journal, Feb. 26, 1921

42 Dunkirk Evening Observer, Oct. 22, 1921

43 Ogdensburg Republican Journal, March 11, 1921

44 Ogdensburg Republican Journal, Dec. 5, 1921

45 Ogdensburg Republican Journal, Dec. 5, 1921

46 Massena Observer, April 21, 1921

47 Victoria Daily Times, Victoria, B.C. April 1, 1924

48 The Post Star, Glens Falls, N.Y. Dec. 10, 1936

49 Massena Observer, April 28, 1921

50 Massena Observer, April 21, 1921

51 Ogdensburg Republican Journal, April 11, 1921

52 Detroit Free Press, July 29, 1921

53 Ogdensburg Republican Journal, April 11, 1921

54 Potsdam Courier, April 13, 1921

55 Massena Observer, April 14, 1921

56 Massena Observer, Feb. 28, 1921

57 Chateaugay Record, March 11, 1921

58 Malone Farmer, March 21, 1921

59 New York Herald, New York City, April 28, 1921

60 Adirondack News, St. Regis Falls, April 30, 1921

61 Adirondack News, St. Regis Falls, May 7, 1921

62 Chateaugay Record, May 13, 1921

63 Chateaugay Record, May 27, 1921

64 History of the New York State Police, Website

65 Malone Farmer, June 29, 1921

66 Chateaugay Record, Aug. 12, 1921

67 Ogdensburg Republican Journal, Oct. 13, 1921

68 Ogdensburg Republican Journal, Oct. 12, 1921

69 Ogdensburg Republican Journal, Oct. 13, 1921

70 Ogdensburg Republican Journal, Oct. 14, 1921

71 Ogdensburg Republican Journal, Oct. 14, 1921

72 Ogdensburg Republican Journal, Oct. 13, 1921

73 Ogdensburg Republican Journal, Oct. 14, 1921

74 Ogdensburg Advance and Weekly St. Lawrence Democrat, Oct. 20, 1921

75 Ogdensburg Republican Journal, Oct. 15, 1921

76 Ogdensburg Republican Journal, Oct. 15, 1921

77 Ogdensburg Advance and Weekly St. Lawrence Democrat, Jan. 26, 1922

78 Ogdensburg Republican Journal, Feb. 14, 1921

79 Lake Placid News, Dec. 4, 1924

80 Ogdensburg Republican Journal, Dec. 19, 1921

81 Ogdensburg Republican Journal, Dec. 19, 1921

82 Malone Farmer, July 20, 1921

83 Ogdensburg Republican Journal, April 11, 1921

84 Chateaugay Record and Franklin County Democrat, Nov. 25, 1921

85 Ogdensburg Republican Journal, Dec. 1, 1921

86 Chateaugay Record, Dec. 9, 1921

87 Ogdensburg Republican Journal, Dec. 19, 1921

88 Ogdensburg Republican Journal, Dec. 27, 1921

89 Courier Freeman, Potsdam, Dec. 28, 1921

90 Courier Freeman, Potsdam, Jan. 4, 1922

91 Courier Freeman, Potsdam, Jan. 11, 1921

About The Author

James E. Reagen has been writing about Northern New York and its history for almost four decades. He is a 1974 graduate of Ogdensburg Free Academy. Mr. Reagen began his journalism career at the University of Virginia where he wrote for the Cavalier Daily, the college's award-winning daily student-run newspaper. During the summer of 1976, he spent a week with the White House Press Office, assisting with U.S. President Gerald R. Ford's visit to Thomas Jefferson's home "Monticello" during the July 4th Bicentennial celebration. In 1977, he co-wrote a series of articles on the struggles facing Afri-

JAMES AND DONNA REAGEN

can American students at the University of Virginia which led to the University President resigning from a racially discriminatory country club. The student newspaper won the national Robert F. Kennedy Memorial Journalism Award in 1977 for its coverage. He was invited to the home of Robert F. Kennedy's widow for a cocktail party and attended a luncheon at the Kennedy Center in Washington, D.C. where the award, a bust of Robert F. Kennedy, was presented.

A quarter century later, he was invited to return to the University to speak at a Black Student Alliance sponsored forum to commemorate the award. He was on a panel discussion that talked about how the articles he and others wrote helped the southern college improve the lives of its minority students.

In the spring of 1977, when the University filed charges against student reporters from the Cavalier Daily, Reagen and his co-editors challenged the case in U.S. District Court, leading to their dismissal.

In 1979, he went to work for the Martinsville, Va. Bulletin, a daily newspaper in southside Virginia.

In 1981, he began writing about murders across upstate New York for true crime magazines, including Front Page Detective, Inside Detective and Master Detective Magazines. His articles included such classics as "Who Plugged Johnny YaYa," "Seven Slugs for the Self-Made Man," and "Daylight Found the Bishop Bludgeoned" to name a few.

In 1982, he returned to Northern New York as a reporter for his hometown newspaper, the Ogdensburg Journal and Advance News. He served as editor of the weekly St. Lawrence Plaindealer in Canton, N.Y., before being named Managing Editor of the Ogdensburg Journal and Sunday Advance News in 1984. At the time, he was the youngest daily newspaper editor in New York State. He oversaw the daily operations of the newspaper for 28 years, writing over 10,000 editorials in the Ogdensburg Journal.

Over his career, he was honored with several investigative reporting and spot news deadline writing awards by the New York State Associated Press Managing Editors Association and the New York State Bar Association.

His awards include a First Place Award for In-Depth Reporting for an investigative series on problems in the foster care program; a Second Place Award for investigative reporting for a series of articles on an investigation of a police sergeant accused of burglarizing Ogdensburg businesses, a First Place deadline reporting with the staff of the Ogdensburg Journal and the Massena-Potsdam Daily Courier Observer for team coverage of the FBI raid on illegal casinos operating on the Akwesasne Mohawk Reservation. He was also honored by the New York State Bar Association for his coverage of a child sexual abuse cases involving a town justice.

The newspaper was also cited in the 1980s by the Associated Press for its coverage of a couple who had opened a gay dude ranch who had been driven out of business by armed bigots who threatened their lives. He was the first newspaper editor in Northern New York to support gay rights in the 1980s.

During the Ice Storm of 1998, he was honored by the Associated Press after he and members of the staff of the Journal and the staff of the Massena-Potsdam Courier-Observer published a joint edition of the two newspapers from his dining room table, producing the only newspaper that was available in the first days after the devastating Ice Storm.

In 2011, he went to work for the New York State Senate as the communications director for State Senator Patty Ritchie where he was employed for 12 years.

He is the author of four other books, a novel, Wizardry, the League of the Crimson Crescent; Warriors of La Presentation, a history of the French and Indian War; Fort Oswegatchie, a history of

Northern New York's role in the Revolutionary War; and Booze, Bad-boys & Bootleggers (North Country Tales Grandpa Never Told You. (Volume 1). He also wrote "Tales from the Oswegatchie Delta," a newspaper column on the history of Northern New York.

He has two stepsons, Bill Hosmer of Ogdensburg and Dan Hosmer of Rotterdam, N.Y. He is the proud grandfather of five grandchildren - Penelope, Jack, Jay, Ben, and Emilie. He and his wife, the former Donna Lee Martin, live in Ogdensburg where they own and operate the historic, award-winning bed and breakfast, the Sherman Inn.

He is a recipient of the Paul Harris Award from the Ogdensburg Rotary Club; a recipient of the Seaway Festival Committee's Jay Cole Award; and Ogdensburg Command Performances Franky Award.

He is a founding member of the Fort La Presentation Association, the Ogdensburg Historic Commission, and the Ogdensburg Museum Committee. He also helped develop Founders Day Weekend and the annual winter Battle of Ogdensburg.

He chaired Ogdensburg's War of 1812 Downtown Battlefield Commission.

In 2018, and again in 2022, during a very polarized political era, he was elected to the St. Lawrence County Legislature to represent Ogdensburg with bipartisan support.

He serves on the St. Lawrence County Industrial Development Agency helping local businesses to expand and recruit new companies to locate in Northern New York.

He is a member of the Ogdensburg Kiwanis Club, serving as Advisor to the Ogdensburg Free Academy Key Club, an award-winning high school service club, for over 32 years. The New York District Key Club awarded him the Key to Honor for his service to New York State's young people. He is also a recipient of the Ogdensburg Kiwanis Club's Kiwanian of the Year.

In 2019, the Ogdensburg City School System presented him with its Civic Award for his contributions to the community's young people. He was also invited to speak at the Ogdensburg Free Academy Senior Class Academic recognition night.

One of his proudest accomplishments as Managing Editor of the Ogdensburg Journal and Advance News was advocating for the cleanup of Lighthouse Point and helping to force Exxon Mobil to conduct the $10 million cleanup that has made it into a major historical attraction for the Ogdensburg community. In 2023, he was presented the Persis Boyesen Award by the Fort La Presentation Association for his years of effort on behalf of the organization.

www.ingramcontent.com/pod-product-compliance
Lightning Source LLC
Chambersburg PA
CBHW060915120626
46553CB00001B/334